TOMORROW'S COMPETITION

Other AMACOM Books by Mack Hanan:

Competing on Value (With Peter Karp)
Consultative Selling™ (Fourth Edition)
Customer Satisfaction (With Peter Karp)
If You Don't Have a Plan, Stay in the Car
Key Account Selling (Second Edition)
Outperformers™ (With Tim Haigh)
Recompetitive Strategies
Successful Market Penetration

TOMORROW'S COMPETITION

The Next Generation of Growth Strategies

Mack Hanan

amacom
American Management Association

This publication is designed to provide accurate and authoritative
information in regard to the subject matter covered. It is sold with
the understanding that the publisher is not engaged in rendering
legal, accounting, or other professional service. If legal advice or
other expert assistance is required, the services of a competent
professional person should be sought.

Library of Congress Cataloging-in-Publication Data

Hanan, Mack.
    Tomorrow's competition : the next generation of growth strategies
    / Mack Hanan.
      p.   cm.
    Includes index.
    ISBN 0-8144-5063-6 (hardcover)
    ISBN 0-8144-7862-X (pbk.)
    1. Competition. 2. Strategic planning.   I. Title.
HD41.H28   1991   91-53057
658.4'012—dc20   CIP

First AMACOM paperback edition 1993.

Printing number

10   9   8   7   6

To
Jim Sweeney,
who skipped over today
by bringing tomorrow's competition
into yesterday's world

Contents

The Challenge of
the Man From Shell

The Man From Shell looked out at his audience. It was made up of his company's top vendors, many of long standing and all of high repute. "I will take exactly three minutes of your time," he said, "because I have only three things to say.

"One, I want to congratulate all of you on your quality. Each of you should be proud of your products; we are. On a scale of 1 to 10, I would rank each of you a 10 or close to it. You leave us little to differentiate between you on quality.

"Two, I want to congratulate all of you on your service. Each of you should be proud of your service—training, maintenance, replacement, and repair—we are. On the same scale of 1 to 10, I would rank each of you a 10 or close to it. As with your products, you leave us little to differentiate between you on service.

"Now, number three. In spite of the first two things I have said—or maybe because of them—we will probably not be doing business with 90 percent or more of you any longer. It is simply too expensive for us to send out dozens of requests for proposals, assess each of them, negotiate them down cut by cut, and subsidize a large staff to spend its time on what has become essentially a repetitive operation. Nor can we have our people take the time to have five, ten, fifteen salespeople from each of your organizations, each representing a separate department or division or even a single product line, call on them every day even when there is no good business reason to do so. In addition, we cannot go on supporting the internal costs of training and retraining our own people when we buy from multiple vendors who have different methods or systems for getting what turns out to be basically similar results. In order to economize, we need to standardize.

"Finally, even though all of you try hard to understand our business, none of you really knows it well enough—and it will get harder, not easier, as we grow here, downsize there, diversify into new businesses, and divest out of others—and we have no good way to teach it to all of you: not the time, not the talent to devote to it, and not the inclination.

"As a result, we are going to choose one or two suppliers from each major category of our needs and make strategic alliances with them and take them deep into our business as our long-term growth partners. We will make our choices on the basis of who among you gives us the most compelling reason. Thank you."

"Wait!" everyone shouted at once. "What is a compelling reason why you should partner with us?"

For the first time, The Man From Shell smiled. "Now at last you're asking the right question."

I

Tomorrow's Winning Challenge

1

The New Golden Rule of Competition

What will it take to win tomorrow's competition? You will have to pledge allegiance to a new golden rule: *Make your business competitive by making the businesses of your customers more competitive.*

Companies that believe that "the future is now" are already competing by making their customers more advantaged. These companies are helping customers become lower-cost manufacturers and higher-margin or higher-share marketers. They are learning how to be their customers' strategic business allies rather than alternate vendors. Instead of simply selling to customers, tomorrow's competitors are helping customers operate their business functions and processes more cost-effectively and taking over many of the operations as co-managers or outsourcers. They are focusing narrowly on dominating major market segments and seeking to dominate them as their industry standard of value. It is sometimes difficult to find out what their products are because they leave them in the car when they call on customers. In their place, they feature the value of the financial impact that their products and services can have on a customer's competitiveness, and they make their price a function of their value.

By using tomorrow's strategies today, companies are committing themselves to the belief that the competitiveness of their customers is the only guarantor of their own competitiveness. Without customers whose businesses are growing, they know that there will be no basis for their own growth. All the technology in the world, all the world's records for quality, and all of the now-shopworn searches for excellence will avail them nothing. They will simply be high-tech, high-quality seekers of excellence that have become competitively disadvantaged.

In order to be a winner in tomorrow's competition, you must plan far beyond such policy statements as "What has carried us through the 1980s is not going to carry us through the 1990s" and leave it at that or, in the words of Goodyear Tire & Rubber Company—in 1985, leader of the world tire market but by 1990 only one of five companies that held three-quarters of the market—"We cannot go to the market the way we have the last fifty years."

Economies of scale, continual operational decentralizing and progressive flattening of management hierarchies until they become Frisbee-thin, and emphasis on "total" quality control—management practices that have become popular in the recent past—will only get you to the dance. If you want to high-step, you will have to go along with Jon Madonna, chairman of the Big Six accounting firm KPMG Peat Marwick, who is downsizing his business because "biggest no longer implies best. . . . Growth for the sake of growth—in numbers of any kind other than profitability—has gone the way of many other tenets of the seventies and eighties." Peat's partnership is being slimmed down because "some of our partners don't have the skillset needed in today's world. Handshakes with clients aren't enough. We need to help them improve their profit margins."

Tomorrow's competition marks the end of the era of a business history dominated by the struggle between advocates of products and technologies versus markets on the one hand and volume and profits on the other as the drive forces for business growth. Market ideology and profit primacy have won. Their victory is becoming so overwhelming that there will no longer be any real contention between them. Anyone who does not catch on will never catch up.

Acknowledging the Decade of the Customer

If your company is still stuck "in history," imitating the business models of the past that worked when you and your industry were young, you may not emerge from the 1990s or be recognizable when you do.

Hewlett-Packard Company is an example of what Dean Morton of its chief executive office calls "a business model based on an old paradigm." Essentially an engineer-driven test and measurement instruments manufacturer, the company got into computers, but it never got into the businesses of the customers who drive computer sales. It tried combining its two businesses, then separating them and atomizing the computer business along product lines that picked their competitors unwisely and "concentrated" on what its marketing people once boasted were over ninety market segments. As a result, priorities were diffuse and ever-changing and duplications of effort were rampant. New-wave curves were regularly missed in growth markets due to old-wave focus on cutting and recutting the business into product-based parts and paying profitless attention to markets where there was only a tiny presence and little prospective opportunity to develop it.

Hewlett-Packard's entire management team matured in parallel, reaching their fifties within thirty years or so of service as the 1990s began. Inbred, with their cumulative management memories gridlocked back in the 1960 era, they encouraged perpetual internal debate on optimal engineering solutions to computer operations while major competitors and customers were satisfied with optimizing business solutions to customer operating problems. Because HP's engineers have always been exceedingly creative, their formidable opposing views often neutralized each other to the point where what John Young, HP's long-time chief executive officer, called "the problem of being late" turned technically excellent products into mature commodities even before they made their market entry.

While all this was going on, HP's marketing people were distributing questionnaires that asked for responses of twenty-five words or less to the question, "Is HP a truly market-oriented

company?" The most meaningful answers came from HP's customers themselves, who were buying on discounted prices that
were between 40 and 50 percent off rather than on compelling
value. The combination of such low to nonexistent margins with
high R&D reinvestment, which bespeaks the classical market
disorientation, locates the epicenter of HP's management mind-
set deep in the 1960–1980 generation, the prehistory of tomorrow's competition.

This is not a problem of failing to learn from history but of
failing to emerge from it. The 1990s will be an increasingly
unforgiving decade for history dwellers. Competitors will not
forgive you as readily as they used to by imitating your errors—
those you either commit or omit. Customers will not forgive you
for failing to satisfy their needs for competitive advantage. They
will tell you, as a spokesperson for Buick once told the president
of its advertising agency Kudner, "What a helluva guy you are"
and then, after doing business with you, as Buick did with
Kudner for a quarter of a century or more, fire you and switch
their business to someone else. Your shareholders and the investment community will not forgive you for not adding either to
their value or to yours and will get even with you by assigning
low multiples of earnings to your equities. And you will have a
hard time forgiving yourself for lost opportunities to grow your
business by growing the businesses of your customers. If you
wake up every morning the way Hewlett-Packard once did—to
"kill DEC," one of its major competitors, Digital Equipment
Company,—instead of to grow your customers, you will be
getting up on the wrong side of the bed.

Tomorrow's competition will unmistakably reveal the true
source of wealth creation. It will be clear that your customers and
only your customers can make wealth for you and that every
supplier's wealth is second-derivative wealth, derived from customers. In order to become wealthy, you must grow your customers so that they can maximize their ability to grow not only
themselves but you, their supplier, as well. In the past, management attention has been mostly focused on the creation of higher
value-added products and services. Tomorrow, you will have to
become a *higher value-adding supplier* so that your customers will
be able to act as *higher value-adding suppliers* to you in return.

Making New-Wave Resolutions

The strategies for winning tomorrow's competition have originated in the self-assessments that observant managers have been
making of their businesses as they have taken them through
booms and busts, upsizings and downsizings, buy-ins and spinouts. They have seen competitive advantages equalize in almost
every industry, R&D fail to be an ever-normal source of commercializable breakthroughs, and global competitors make a mockery
of "barriers to entry" to eradicate the old established boundaries
between price and performance. They have experienced the introduction of customer standards of quality and interchangeability
of operations that have obsoleted their own proprietary standards; they have also seen the rising importance of third-party
distribution channels as ways of reaching out and touching their
customers directly, often to their own exclusion; and finally, they
have realized the costly curse of being stuck way back on the
manufacturing and processing end of the value chain.

They have learned what it is like to be technology-rich with
no sense of a market and what it is like to be heavy with both the
capital and the human assets of bureaucracy—with no entrepre-
neurialism, flexibility, or innovation. They have discovered what
it is like to miss a new product curve and try to play catch-up and
what it is like to be more than slightly ahead of their time. They
have watched their managers invest hundreds of millions of
dollars in technology, and only after the fact did they become
ruefully aware of how much more attention should have been
paid to evolving new strategies that would be customer-enhancing rather than simply computer-enhanced.

The single common conclusion managers like these have
come to is that the upshots of these experiences are simply
unaffordable when carried over into the future. They are unaffordable in terms of their cost. They are also unaffordable in the
market opportunities that are lost because of them, the emergent
businesses that get thrown out with the bathwater, and the
growth that is denied all around when a product or a business or
an industry—or a nation—defaults on fulfilling its potential.

The strategists for tomorrow all share this common denominator of guarding against unaffordability. No one, they resolve, can any longer afford to do, or allow to happen, any of the following:

- Compete unpartnered.
- Sell on price and performance.
- Maintain cost centers.
- Go it alone in R&D.
- Bet incorrectly on the next technology.
- Manufacture full lines.
- Market products horizontally.
- Maintain inventory.
- Own capital equipment.
- Buy from multiple vendors.
- Let third parties come between you and your customers.
- Allow customers to grow slowly or not at all.

Standardizing Market Consciousness

The market genesis of every business has become gospel. The market sourcing of business strategy will be forever the central theme of management science. Product- or process-centered models of how business works—the old "better mousetrap" theories—have become defunct because their adherents cannot compete. Given the daily reality in industry after industry of the products of breakthrough technology selling at discounted margins from the moment of their introduction, the old models have nowhere further to go.

Attaching price to a product or process instead of to the customer value it creates has proved over and over again to be the kiss of death to profitability. Customer values, not product values, have come to be the key to margins. Market consciousness, not the consciousness of product features and benefits, has become the universal business standard for making, selling, and pricing value. With customers now regularly being brought in to mutual profit-improving partnerships with their suppliers, and suppliers partnering with each other for the same reason, no further struggle about where the center of a business is located will be productive because no ideology can go head to head with market genesis and win.

Companies that are already competing as if it were tomorrow are proposing their value in terms of improved customer profits and warranting its fulfillment: not just "your money back if not satisfied" but your profits enhanced. They are circumventing competitors by managing the customer facilities and categories they sell to in order to preempt comparative product decisions.

Many of these companies are acting on the belief that the best way to win a Malcolm Baldrige National Quality Award for themselves may be to help a customer win one first. They are rewarding their people on the basis of the bottom line of customer satisfaction instead of solely on the basis of the satisfaction of the managers who review them and to whom they report. Companies like these are already out there, practicing and perfecting the strategies of tomorrow. The standards of performance they set will be the ones to beat, if you can.

Other companies, meanwhile, are "thinking about" the effects that such departures from traditional business practice might have on their cultures. "What if we do?" they are asking themselves when they should be asking, "What if we don't?"

Well into the coming years vestiges of past competition will exist as present-day incarnations of the old Baldwin Locomotive Works, which tried to get one more generation out of steam power in an emerging age of electricity, or Lockheed, which tried to get one more generation out of piston power early in the age of jets. There will still be companies like the predivestiture AT&T, whose inventive genius outran its marketing ability with the Picturephone, as happened at Du Pont with Corfam and at Corning, where development people produced the first light-reactive photochromic lenses but then marketing people forgot to brand them. Companies like ITT will still exist, where centralization at the top stifled entrepreneurial autonomy everywhere below, and Hewlett-Packard, where autonomy without centralized leadership has brought about corporationwide anomie, team-by-team duplication of work, redundancy of resources, and a need for a matrix of horizontal consensus and vertical approvals that quadruples and quintuples decision-making time and discourages action.

There will be companies whose top managers will still be practicing "wandering around management" in their own offices but who will see their customers' operations, if at all, mainly from the offices of their top-management "old boy" peers. There will still be companies that train their sales forces to seek out "coaches" inside customer companies who may teach them where, how, and to whom to sell instead of positioning themselves as their customers' coaches and teaching customer managers how to improve their competitive advantage.

There will be companies like Apollo and Wang Laboratories, who possess the breakthrough skills to create genuinely new markets but end up giving them away because all they can supply are products whose technology is quickly equalized and so their margins cannot be sustained.

There will be companies like Merrill Lynch and GTE and United Technologies that are dominated for so long by a single chief executive that no singular successors, who represent the next generation's business vision, are encouraged to flourish, and so as a result an inevitable void occurs. Such companies will still be remaking history. As they "sell harder" and repeatedly "go back to basics" in combating tomorrow's customer-driven competition, they will come into head-on conflict with businesses that have already completed their evolution into the "common marketization" of competition. Among these "common market companies," the ideology of making customers more competitive will be the sole basis for business.

Embracing Tomorrow's Critical Success Factors

For each added year that you and your managers remain devoted to your products and processes, you will fall farther behind the power curve of the competitive edge as your rivals pull ahead in consolidating growth partnerships with the most growable and fastest-growing customers and suppliers. It is not simply a question of your market share. It is your growth-partner share that will be at risk, as the best partners become engaged. Without good growers among your customers and suppliers, who will grow you?

Certain industries seem to have a genetic code that predisposes them to remain locked in the past, believing that they are competing and being competitive when they are no longer either addressing their markets or redressing their competitors. If you are in a technology-based business in electronics, such as computer and telecommunications systems, or a science-based business such as biotechnology, biomedicine, instrumentation, or health care, you are at major risk. So are capital equipment businesses of all sorts and process industries in such fields as petroleum and chemicals. If a business "smokes"—that is, if it has plants and factories—it enlarges its competitive risk. If it is overweight with full product lines, multiple unniched mass markets, and vertically integrated operating units, its risk is multiplied severalfold. And if it is astigmatic, focusing its vision inward on the perfectability of its products to the exclusion of perfecting the competitiveness of its customers, it will be blindsided by other more market-derived businesses with well-developed customer connections.

The dynamics of change in most industries move slowly, outmoding businesses and ways of doing business "while you wait." In mid-1991, Chairman John Akers of IBM diagnosed some of the symptoms of being stuck in the past that he could no longer ignore in his own company: "The fact that we're losing market share makes me goddam mad. . . . Everyone is too comfortable at a time when the business is in crisis."

Worldwide sales of IBM hardware, software, and services had dropped almost 15 percent in the ten years up to 1991. Operating profit margins had taken an even greater fall. While margins had gone down as the computer industry matured, costs had gone up, sales growth had slowed, new products were coming out slow and late, and customer needs were still not making it into technology. Meantime comparisons told the story in a nutshell. IBM mainframes had a 3.5 month meantime between failures, while Hitachi mainframes went over 24 months; IBM disk drives went down every 2.5 months, while Fujitsu's rate was more than 12 months.

Business Week asked a number of management "gurus" what Akers should do next. With their reiterations of the platitudes and soothsayings of the 1980s and even earlier, they turned out to be equally stuck in history along with the man they were asked to help. Amory Houghton, Jr., former CEO of Corning, Inc., thought it would be sufficient to "Rattle the cage. Shake them up." Irving Shapiro, who failed to solve many of the same problems as CEO of Du Pont, still believes in "Better things for better living through chemistry: Everything has to turn on R&D." With gurus like that, John Akers does not need Hitachi and Fujitsu.

Tomorrow's critical success factors are tightly focused on hooking up each of your businesses to its market's drive for competitive advantage. Six of these factors will be supercritical because they are the best ways of making customers advantaged:

1. As businesses globalize, raising competition to new and more exacting levels, tomorrow's managers will have to master the art of creating compelling visions of their enterprises as enhancers of the competitive advantage of their customers rather than as manufacturers, processors, suppliers, or vendors.

2. As leadership becomes more consensual, more diffused and decentralized within compressed organization structures, tomorrow's managers will have to master the ability to negotiate agreements as a peer and partner, working laterally rather than from the top down in order to guarantee their achievement.

3. As markets become increasingly specialized and more finitely segmented, tomorrow's managers will have to master the ability to compete vertically in order to become market specialists in expanding their customers' competitiveness.

4. As products become more difficult to differentiate and as customers demand solutions based on common performance denominators, multivendor compatability, and open standards, tomorrow's managers will have to master the ability to compete on the basis of customer value rather than product value in order to avoid margin erosion.

5. As resources become costlier to use and misuse and as the technologies for their implementation become more sophisti-cated, tomorrow's managers will have to master the ability to cooperate with other suppliers in order to share the brainpower

and financial burdens of commercializing successive waves of innovations.

6. As customers concentrate on defining and managing their core strategic businesses, tomorrow's managers will have to master the ability to compete by outsourcing customer support operations in order to convert them from cost centers into cost-effective operations.

The net result of these strategies will be to make customers the focal point of the way you manage your business. The old corporate nationalism that proclaimed "We are the best" to anyone who would listen will give way to collaborative partnering whose testimony will be "We make our customers the best."

To win in this environment, you will need a set of counter-priorities:

• Instead of asking your managers to predict tomorrow, an arcane talent at best and not necessarily correlated with the ability to run a business, ask your major customers to quantify their growth objectives and put your managers to work to help contribute to them.

• Instead of amusing yourself on retreats by concocting "bands of possibilities" for futuristic scenarios, create joint growth plans with your customers that are likely to strengthen each customer's competitiveness.

• Instead of saying, "We never want to lose a customer because we don't have the technology," grow your customers as the best way to avoid losing them and feel free to acquire emerging technologies or integrate them into your business as they are needed.

• Instead of coveting technologies, remember that the major added values are always found in the application of a technology rather than in its manufacture. Nor should you covet asset building—being the biggest at anything—remembering that the least costly asset is always the one you do not have to own.

2

Competing in a Megaworld

Tomorrow's competition will be dominated by multibusiness, multinational megacorps. In every industry, one or two of them will be the major players. Each will be composed of multiple lines of business and layer upon layer of strategic allies in the form of cooperative partnerships with other megacorps, joint ventures and minority investments with smaller companies, and buy-instead-of-make relationships with outsourcers. In many industries, 1.8 megacorps will be enough. There will be little need for a number 2 and no need at all for a number 3.

If you manage a megacorp or plan to grow your business to become one, you must do everything you can to become your industry's number 1. This means you must capitalize on the strengths of megasize and counteract the impacts of the weaknesses that go along with them.

If you manage a small or mid-size business—a microcorp or a minicorp—that competes against megacorps, you must capitalize on the strengths inherent in your own size and the weaknesses of your smaller or larger competitors. Whatever your size, the best growers of your commonly held customers will win.

Tomorrow's megacorps will be bigger than ever. Fewer megacorps of great power will therefore dominate each industry. They will set the industry tone and texture. No one will be able to ignore them. But they will also set the tone and texture of the companies that challenge them. Wherever megacorps are weak, their competitors will be many and strong.

While megacorps are gaining increased monopoly power over the things they make and market, they are also becoming major financial institutions rivaling banks and brokerages and insurance companies. The credit and finance subsidiaries of Ford Motor Company, General Motors Corporation, and AT&T already issue their own money market accounts as alternatives to bank money market accounts and money market mutual funds. Investments in Ford and AT&T are so far available only to employees. General Motors and IBM make their accounts more widely available.

Megacorps are further extending their power by teaming up. IBM has alliances with MCI Communications, Martin Marietta, Boeing, and NYNEX for joint participation in complex integrated computer and telecommunications systems. IBM is also teaming up with some of its largest customers, such as Texaco, to remarket IBM computer applications to other companies in each of its customer's markets.

No industry will be immune from megacorp supremacy:

• In automobile retailing, the traditional single franchise holder is being superseded by the megadealer. Where once a dealer of the Big Three could sell only two of the same manufacturer's car lines, megadealers now operate as many as forty to fifty franchises that sell thirty-five domestic and imported makes. By the late 1980s, 5 percent of these consolidated dealerships were already selling 30 percent of all cars.

• Food, drug, and hardware retailers are coming together in one-stop-shopping "hypermarkets" that sometimes contain over five acres of shopping space for their combined supermarket and discount wares. Known as "malls without walls," they sell everything from tulips to turnips to television sets. Each store serves an average of 50,000 shoppers a week who spend between $100 and $200 million a year.

• The American financial system has also entered the mega-corp era with superbanks and nationwide financial conglomerates. As a result of mergers, takeovers, and failures, many traditional banks and savings institutions have disappeared along with dozens of brokerage houses and insurance companies. The survivors have evolved into financial supermarkets. Tomorrow's competitors will be led by huge financial institutions that offer every conceivable financial service. By the year 2000, there could be only ten to twenty world-class banks, each trading twenty-four hours a day in multibillion dollar transactions. Megabanks like these will be the financial mass merchandisers of the world. Meanwhile, hundreds of microbanks will be competing against them on the basis of specialized products, personal attention, and small-town type service.

• In advertising, mega-agencies have come about to take advantage of the increasing centralization of media and the explosion of decentralized television programming options. Giant media companies with global reach and new communications technologies such as videotex and cable TV have expanded the options for delivering news and entertainment vehicles for advertising. Tomorrow's advertising will be vested in an agency's ability to place advertising worldwide by customizing it everywhere based on a common theme. When mega-agencies grow to a size that threatens their creativity, many of them subcontract their work to microboutique outsourcers composed of small, highly specialized copy and art groups.

• In magazine advertising sales, advertisers are being asked to contract for ads in systems of integrated magazines instead of buying advertising on a magazine-by-magazine basis. Megapublishers like Time Warner, Hearst, and Meredith are selling their multimagazine systems as a form of "asset synergy" for advertisers who go "all Meredith," for example, in order to address normally separate cross-media audiences.

• The computer software business has come to be dominated by two kinds of retailers: huge megastores that emphasize low prices across a broad-based selection and microboutiques that stock one type of software in depth and specialize in service to a single-niche market. Stores that do not fit either of these categories, referred to as hybrids, are being squeezed between the high-volume superstores and the specialty niche players. The margins tell the story—30 percent for the specialty microstores versus 12 to 22 percent for the hybrid ministores.

• The airline industry has consolidated into a handful of megacarriers that will dominate international air travel. These superlines have a stranglehold on the most valuable routes, airport slots, and computerized reservation systems that put second-tier minilines at a competitive disadvantage. The only niche players left will be the commuter airlines that serve the megacarriers' hubs. But they too are disadvantaged without alliances with the largest carriers. As David Hinson, chairman of Midway Airlines, said when the megacarriers drove him out of his Philadelphia hub, "The large get larger. Only smaller players who have specialty niches can play."

Narrowing the Range of Choice

The concentration of sources of supply into the hands of a shrinking number of megacorps is narrowing the choices for everyone who deals with them as well as for megacorps themselves. In some industries where megacorps predominate, competition is already becoming effectively owned by dedicated, exclusive partnerships. In the photographic supply and amusement park businesses, for example, Walt Disney and Eastman Kodak have made a fifteen-year agreement that gives Disney cartoon characters exposure in Kodak advertising in return for Kodak becoming the sole supplier of cameras and film at Disney theme parks. No one but Kodak can sell film at Disneyworld. No one else in the photography business can use Mickey Mouse.

Many large apparel retailers are decreasing the number of vendors they deal with by increasing their private label merchandise. This enables stores to limit their buying to a smaller number of large manufacturers who sell them a mix of both nationally branded clothes and the same or similar merchandise that carries the stores' own labels.

In publishing, the small players are being progressively excluded from access to the distribution systems controlled by megacorp retailers. B. Dalton Bookseller, the number 2 retail chain in the United States, has established a minimum annual sales volume as an entry fee to get books on its stores' shelves. A publisher who sells less than $100,000 worth of books a year with Dalton will be denied exposure of its titles in Dalton's almost 800 stores.

When a small number of major customers deal mostly with a small number of major suppliers, a constructive monopoly exists. This is the situation in the medical diagnostic-imaging business. Hospitals in the United States and abroad have only five mega-corp suppliers to choose from: General Electric in the United States; the merged Philips-General Electric in Europe; Siemens A. G. in West Germany; and two Japanese companies, Hitachi and Toshiba. Before they combined, N. V. Philips and GE of Britain were already megacorps but were still unable to make it in the big leagues on their own. In the United States, even a megacorp the size of Johnson & Johnson has had to drop out of the medical-imaging business. General Electric has made itself even stronger at J&J's expense, buying its inventories and service commitments.

Megacorp dog is eating megacorp dog. It is the same in every industry where business options are rapidly being consolidated in the hands of a few companies.

In the hotel industry, twenty-five companies currently control about 50 percent of all rooms. Sometime in the 1990s, three or four of these companies will come to dominate the market. The best performers, the megachains with the lowest median pretax loss per room, will absorb the rest.

In the computer industry, a handful of megasuppliers will control 75 percent of sales in the 1990s. They will be principally facility managers and systems integrators, providing an all-encompassing management of customized, integrated computer networks containing multimanufactured products.

Industries like these will become oligarchies of megacorps. Just as in the past when steel was dominated by U.S. Steel, automobiles by General Motors, and tires by Goodyear, tomorrow's oligarchies will support each other's prices and policies. Major customers will have little choice but to go to them. When they do, they will find they have little or no choice among their undifferentiated terms and conditions, let alone products and services. The same shoe fits the other foot as well. Megacorp suppliers will find they have little or no choice among their megacorp customers' undifferentiated "open standard" purchase specifications.

The initial savings through not having to shop around will often be canceled out by loss of the savings normally afforded by competitive choice. For many megacorps, the logical next step has already been taken. Suppliers and customers are entering into dedicated long-term agreements to buy and sell with each other. Each pairing works out its own basis for doing business. The buying company generally becomes intimately involved with its supplier's product development, manufacturing, and inventory control processes while the selling company becomes equally intimate with the buyer's operating processes it sells into and the buyer's markets on which both buyer and supplier sales depend. The buyer may even turn out to be a reseller of the supplier's products to its own markets.

In a practical sense, megamarriages like these will do away with traditional competitive bidding, buying, and selling. A supplier's applications experts will be long-term residents in his buyer's operations. In turn, the buyer's manufacturing and sales experts will be resident in his supplier's operations. They will work from a joint annual to triennial plan, integrating their related people and processes in a way that will replicate a self-contained independent business.

Downsizing Before You Have To

Maturity comes to megacorp businesses seemingly "all at once," as Du Pont said about its discovery in the 1980s that many of its long-lived commodity products had simultaneously reached "the end of the rainbow." Like most megacorps, Du Pont had stayed with its base businesses too long and had resisted downsizing its assets for years after the handwriting was on the wall. Drags like these on your profits will be intolerable if you manage a megacorp in tomorrow's competition.

Du Pont waited until 1985 to get out of the methanol business, although margins had been steadily decreasing for over two decades. Since 1981 alone, prices had fallen 35 percent. Everyone knew that there were too many suppliers. But everyone also knew that the departure of one big one would improve the profitability of the others that stayed in. No one wanted to be the one who got out. But finally managers at Du Pont calculated that "we can purchase methanol now for less than we can produce it."

If Du Pont had acted sooner, it would have freed itself from its methanol burden sooner. But its century-old executive committee "kept the gate" for all important decisions. Everything had to be run past it. It took until 1990 to abolish it, when Chairman Edgar Woolard, Jr., finally reasoned that "if you don't have an executive committee, you don't have to run it past them." Du Pont has also decided to remove the word *department* from its corporate vocabulary because "if Joe Blow in polymers had a good idea, fibers wouldn't pick it up and run with it." Either fibers would never know or, if it did, it would take a "not invented here" attitude.

Nonetheless, Du Pont's "methanol syndrome" pervades all megacorps. The same delayed reactions have also been endemic at Xerox. For a decade and a half, starting in 1959 with the pioneering model 914, Xerox owned the plain-paper copier market. Its name became the synonym for office copiers. Then, partly as a result of its own success, market growth slowed for large copiers. Xerox had become mature. But its megacorp mind-set remained unchanged.

Instead of thinking small, Xerox refused to consider niche markets of less than $100 million a year in gross revenues. As a result, it abdicated the low end of the copier business, especially personal copiers, to the Japanese. Because of the same mass-market focus, Xerox had also turned down several major new products developed for it by its Palo Alto Research Center that have later proved highly successful for other companies, Apple Computer among them, that became Xerox competitors. Lacking new copier products, Xerox tried to migrate into electronic data systems. In the period 1974–1984, it became the computer industry's most conspicuous failure, losing hundreds of millions of dollars on unmarketable word processors, printers and facsimile transmission machines, filing systems, and computer work stations for the "office of the future."

Xerox has also tried countercyclical diversification, buying into the financial services industry through a $1.5 billion acquisition in property and casualty insurance. Now, in addition to competing against the Japanese in copiers and against IBM in office automation, Xerox is in a third highly competitive industry that is also mature.

Unable to build successful businesses beyond its original copier franchise, Xerox has tried downsizing by reducing costs through layoffs, increasing automation, and outsourcing components to cheaper foreign suppliers. At the same time, it has added to its asset base by stepping up its investment in "exciting products" for office automation. It has been earning less money while spending more money, the classic bind of a mature megacorp.

From 1984 through 1990, Honeywell was in a continuous "rightsizing" mode. In six rounds of write-offs in less than six years, Honeywell sold its mainframe computer and defense businesses and bought a sick aerospace and aviation systems business at excessive cost from Unisys, whose underlying problems Honeywell failed to discover for eighteen months. Honeywell's restructuring turned into a long, drawn-out process. "If you begin to change something as large as Honeywell," its management said, "it's very difficult to do that all at one time." Meanwhile, the company lost sight of its core businesses of home and building controls and industrial automation that account for nearly half of its sales. The controls business, in which Honeywell pioneered, suffered from being "the oldest son on the farm, plowing the back forty and not visible."

When megacorps gets into trouble during recessionary contractions, they see their businesses for what they really are: cost centers that have grown fat in the good times. In 1991, Procter & Gamble Company cut back millions of dollars worth of "nonessential spending" for sales, marketing, and product development. P&G announced that "everyone has been told to figure out their one or two big projects and focus on them and get rid of the rest." Funds would be available only for "the most profitable brands in each category"; unprofitable brands would be in danger of being sold. Yet as soon as business turns around, the 80-20 rule is forgotten, and the race for incremental revenues and market share typically goes on.

In 1989 the commerical aircraft division of McDonnell Douglas, by then number 3 to Boeing and Airbus Industrie, underwent a "Monday morning massacre." Four of nine fatty layers of management were removed from the organization chart, 2,000 job slots disappeared, and all managers were required to reapply for their own positions or become excessed. With an overall profit margin of 1.2 percent, less than half its industry average, the company underwent "a Chinese water torture of write-offs" in an attempt to restructure its commercial business into what it called "either the greatest success story in the history of industrial America or the greatest failure."

Kodak is another megacorp that stayed too long with its internal power structure, its manufacturing methods, and its ways of dealing with suppliers and customers. It waited until the late 1980s to dismantle its huge manufacturing and marketing staffs, decentralize into business units led by general managers who are responsible for costs and profits, and begin to joint venture and outsource all over the world. Long known as the Great Yellow Father, ponderous and paternalistic, Kodak is working to condense its product development cycles and break through its ostrichlike insularity. Copiers have been one of its ostrich eggs. In the 1960s Kodak's technology could have given Xerox a run for the dry copier market. Instead, not wanting to be first out of the box, Kodak spent ten years putting what it said were finishing touches on its machines.

Outsourcing When You Need To

One way to downsize is to outsource, to make the make-or-buy decision in favor of buying. Almost without exception, large businesses have historically adopted a vertical integration of their capabilities. They have self-manufactured most if not all of their required components and ingredients, processing them in their own mills, plants, and factories.

In the eras before global competition, the costs and inefficiencies of in-house vertical business units could either be made up elsewhere, passed along, or absorbed. Now they are no longer affordable. Even traditionally verticalized megacorps are disintegrating, farming out, spinning out, or selling off operations. As systems integration and customer-facility management increase, megacorp managers will realize that they no longer must make everything they sell. In tomorrow's megacorps, manufacturing and marketing will become codependent on satisfying customer needs, not simply product quotas.

Up to the 1980s, few companies had been more thoroughly integrated than General Motors. GM used to manufacture almost three-quarters of each car it sold. Ford, too, made over half of its component parts. Before 1980 vertical integration gave both of these megacorps an economic advantage, especially GM, which was its industry's perennial low-cost producer. From 1980 onward, however, lower-cost component suppliers, most of them overseas, have taken away GM's cost advantages one by one.

As a result, GM has been disposing of many of its vertical operations. Yet it still fills almost two-thirds of its needs internally while Toyota relies on in-house sources of supply less than a third of the time. Toyota manages its outsourcing in a two-tier manner, where the first-tier supplier acts as a prime contractor and second-tier suppliers provide individual parts or subsystem components under his management. In some cases, second-tier companies replicate the hierarchy with third-tier subcontracts.

The only direct dealings with Toyota are in the first tier. These principal suppliers become integral members of Toyota's product-development teams. This allows Toyota to relate to a relatively small number of partners, fewer than 300 in most development projects compared to up to 2,500 at General Motors. To lock in the partnership cycle, Toyota design engineers reside at their first-tier suppliers' plants to participate in production planning.

Throughout the multiple-tier network, the relationships between Toyota, its suppliers, and their subsuppliers is cooperative rather than competitive. All of them share the same desire for long-term, stable, and mutually profitable relations.

By disengaging their vertically integrated business units,

megacorps can provide growing opportunities for the reemerg-
ence of these units as specialist microcorps and midsize minicorps. Some of these divested, self-standing businesses will come
about as the result of leveraged buyouts by their managers.
Others will be sold. These smaller companies, once they are
independent, will cluster around the megacorps they serve, much
like a solar system's satellites. A few may grow to become the
day-after-tomorrow's megacorps.

Decentralizing Even if You Don't Want to

One of the most critical success factors for managing a megacorp
will be your ability to approximate the forms and flexibility of
smaller-size organizations. All megacorps will have to take a daily
test where they ask, "Are we adding more value to the businesses
under our control than someone else could add?" Otherwise the
costs of bigness—the costs of complexity, as they are sometimes
known—may come to outweigh the advantages of size and the
economies of scale.

In large corporations, up to 80 percent of their business units
subtract from the values that the other 20 percent bring in. The
returns from these "80 percent" businesses are often lower than
the capital costs tied up in them; that is, the value of their future
cash flows discounted back to their present value is lower than
their cost of capital. Businesses like these add to the costs, not
the profits, of complexity.

B. F. Goodrich is an example of a megacorp whose costs came
to add up unaffordably. Up to the late 1980s, Goodrich was a
major tire manufacturer with minor interests in industrial rubber
products, speciality chemicals, and aerospace. For many years,
as rising sales volume failed to make up for falling profits, "All
we had to run on was our sense of humor," a spokesman for
Goodrich remembers. In 1985 there was not much left to laugh
about. On sales of $3.2 billion, Goodrich lost $26 million as the
automobile business became depressed, replacement tire sales
slowed along with it, and foreign price competition intensified. It
was at that point that Goodrich made a guess that "inside this fat
company was a thin company dying to get out."

Not only was Goodrich fat, it was fat at the top as well as around the middle. Even though it was a multibillion dollar corporation, a Du Pont type of management committee approval was required for all expenditures over $25,000. After many millions of dollars in write-offs, tens of thousands of firings and early retirements, and divestiture of the tire business, Goodrich is a decentralized company composed of microniche businesses whose specialty chemicals and aerospace operations are considered to be tomorrow's crown jewels.

In only four out of sixty-seven industries in the *Business Week* Top 1,000 are the largest megacorps the most profitable on the basis of return on equity. Well over half the time, the largest megacorp runs below its industry's average return on invested capital. Megacorps make money, but have a hard time rescuing earnings from it. As a result, "somewhat small" is becoming "somewhat more beautiful" as flexibility becomes more important than real or imagined economies of scale. Birmingham Steel Corporation, a minimill, can produce a ton of steel with only a third of the labor of competitive megamills. In computers, Compaq Computer Corporation can develop a new model three to five times faster than IBM. Even though megacorp managers are well aware of these disparities, they find it difficult to act small. This provides competitive access to their markets by small niche-type businesses that can take advantage of the strengths of their smallness.

Some large companies try to have it both ways. General Electric fancies itself as a "big company-small company hybrid" that combines a large corporation's resources with a small company's flexibility, autonomy, and hunger—"the best of both." But that still does not make a megacorp's decentralization easy.

When Air Products & Chemicals, Inc., shifted its strategy from manufacturing bulk commodity chemicals to specialties, it had to learn almost from scratch how to do business. In the past, its old batch-order processing system was adequate for shipping railroad-car–size orders to a small number of major customers who could wait one or two weeks for delivery. But the specialty chemicals market is composed of many small-niche customers who need small quantities and frequent just-in-time deliveries. They also want to know at all times where their shipments are, challenging APC with an entirely new meaning of the term *service.*

As soon as a once-monolithic market fractionalizes into multiple micromarkets, mass marketers have no choice but to learn how to be micromarketers. It has been a long time, for example, since there has been anything that could be called "the market for toothpaste." Today, there is not even "the market for Crest toothpaste." It takes six different advertising campaigns to sell Crest to its niche markets of children, adults, ethnic groups such as African Americans and Hispanics, the retail trade on a one-by-one major-retailer basis, and convenience stores.

Megacorps will have to learn to manage this kind of resource diffusion. This means decentralizing profit responsibility three and four levels, not just one or two. It means relaxing the death grip of executive committees and giving managers authority to invest sums up to $25 to $50 million without approval. It means reducing staff to no more than six or seven support people per thousand employees. It means plants of approximately 250 workers so that every worker on the floor can go to the top to fix a problem or fix it himself before it gets too big.

Concentrating Because Your Markets Tell You To

Throughout the 1980s, many megacorps accelerated their innovative decline by diverting an overabundance of their resources to defending declining franchises that were cash cows rather than creating innovations that would have been more productive of future profits, not just cash flows. This creative understretch has caused an innovative gap. As their innovative strength ebbed even while enormous amounts of cash flowed, some of these companies used market share victories as misinterpreted signals that their old powers were still intact and that innovativeness did not have to be fixed because nothing was broken.

As their innovative decline steepened almost all across the board, megacorps tended to concentrate even more of their energies and resources on defense of their breadwinner businesses. Correspondingly, they have presided over a neglect of their technical competitiveness (especially in the highest technologies), their entrepreneurial cultures that were able to hide out in the nooks and crannies of their bureaucracies, and their management education in profitable business growth as an alternative to "bloath."

To counter the deleterious impact of bureaucracy on innovation, megacorps are atomizing into smaller business units. Some, called focus groups, are microsized. Others are being spun out as satellite companies that, like General Motors' Saturn Corporation and Apple Computer's Claris software business, are set up as separate minicorps or even megacorps apart from their megaparents. As these businesses grow, further cell division can take place to atomize them again and again to create generations of decentralized "satellites of satellites."

General Motors has created a spinout of its data processing functions by taking hundreds of its computer networks, which were costing billions of dollars each year to operate, packaging them into Electronic Data Systems, an entrepreneurial data processing company that it acquired, and spinning off 7,000 employees and all their hardware into the separate profit center with its own stock listing. The spun-off EDS is now being used as the basis for growing a new megacorp, both by internal growth and acquisitions.

Spinning off is far from an automatic success. Xerox made that discovery in 1988 when it spun off its ten-year-old Xerox Artificial Intelligence Business Unit into an independent software company called Envos Corporation. Only seven months later Xerox closed it down, saying that "there were too many large expenditures that a small company could not stand." Envos was overstaffed with forty-seven people although it needed only about twelve to fifteen. It had also been overfunded, with a sunk cost base that was unsupportable by its revenues.

Some megacorps are developing rules for spinning out their business units. One rule is that once a unit reaches a size of 1,000 to 1,500 people, it automatically becomes a candidate for separate status. Other megacorps base their separation agreements on a sales volume threshold or a productivity index that combines size and sales and indicates spinout potential as the number of employees rises against a constant or falling volume. This indicates that the need for a renewal of entrepreneurial innovation is at hand.

By enforcing a ceiling on size and a floor on productivity, megacorps are trying to retain or regain the microcorp advantage of single-minded concentration by a focused team of comparatively autonomous, dedicated people. For this reason, most satellites are given the status of wholly owned subsidiary corporations that can make joint ventures with allied businesses, even other satellites, that offer complementary or supplementary products and services. The satellite status may also be a forerunner to divestiture of a business, endowing it with a separate identity that can serve as the basis for a leveraged buyout.

Megacorps are using spinouts to capitalize the market potential of some of their traditional internal service functions such as purchasing, personnel, and industrial relations that have been consolidated in human resources, market research, sales, and research and development departments. These cost-centered service functions can sometimes be converted into profit centers when they are spun out as subsidiary companies.

One of the most popular types of spinout is financial services, sometimes supplemented by an acquisition. In tomorrow's competition, almost every megacorp will own a financial business, as many of them do now, that sells cash generated by credit or other monetary instruments. They will own brokerages in the same way that General Electric owns Kidder, Peabody, or they will profit from the activities of their credit companies the way Ford and General Motors do. Sears is a total financial services company, dealing in credit through retailing and its brokerage and real estate businesses. American Can Company metamorphosed from a mature manufacturing megacorp into a financial services business called Primerica that is composed of specialty retailing, insurance, investment banking, securities brokerage, mortgage banking, and asset management businesses.

This type of diversification is a good deal safer and may be even more profitable than acquiring other megacorps or their divested businesses. As the 1990s began, Philip Morris held about 40 percent of the United States market for cigarettes. Cigarette sales accounted for almost $4 billion worth of profits and yielded a 64 percent rate of return. When the company looked at diversification opportunities away from the declining market that cigarettes represent, the beer and food businesses it acquired had rates of return that were barely at the 6 percent levels. Anheuser-Busch, number 1 in a declining beer market, has had the same problem with only a 5 percent return from diversifying into the food business, which it says it is learning "the hard way."

Innovating Because You Force Yourself To

If you are a megacorp manager, sooner or later you will discover the truth about size and innovation: The larger the business, the harder to innovate. As size increases, management's emphasis moves away from inventing new businesses to supplying existing businesses in the most cost-effective manner and pricing them competitively. Along with bigness come control systems that monitor, measure, and mediate between creative development processes and their sponsors. They delay and discourage implementation and, by requiring consensus before going ahead, often blunt the innovative edge of new ideas and diffuse individual recognition and reward. The rich, high-quality profits that can come only from innovative ways to grow customers—profits from premium unit margins that require neither discounting nor costly protracted sales cycles—go by the board.

All megacorps seem to suffer from similar drawbacks of getting innovations off the drawing boards and into market. Too many people make too many decisions too many times, many of them standing around while trying to get someone at the next level to sign off. People are encouraged to "nonconcur," disagreeing with each other, while specifications are kept open, and disagreements are escalated upward for resolution. With the advent of globalism, new products are often being held back because there is a policy that says they must be introduced in the same form at the same time all over the world.

Megacorps grow primarily by extension, adding to their existing product lines and installed customer base rather than starting up initial product concepts or opening new markets. Novelty is introduced incrementally over time, progressively obsoleting an original invention but not replacing it. The megacorp focus is usually on exploitation, not experimentation.

This may be one reason why megacorps have trouble greenhousing new businesses. Most megacorps start up so-called independent business units (IBUs) in the hope that they will grow into divisions. Very few succeed. IBM has been luckier than the average megacorp. Its PC independent business unit grew to become the $5 billion dollar Entry Systems Division over four years. But other IBUs like Academic Information Systems, Education Systems, Engineering Systems Products, and Finance Systems have all been merged into existing divisions generally within two years after they were formed. The success of the Entry Systems venture makes up for a lot of failures, but only a handful of megacorps can show even one such achievement out of ten.

Nonetheless, the drive to see whether growth enterprises can be created from small specialized seedlings is incessant although cyclical. Colgate-Palmolive has organized the Colgate Venture Company to act as a new business greenhouse. As a separate organization, it is insulated in the manner of a skunk works from parent company bureaucracy. At General Foods, a separate organization called Culinova Group specializes in developing new products for the takeout refrigerated food business. Scott Paper Company has set up a venture group named the Do-It-Yourself Group to develop products for the home handyman market.

As a rule, megacorps are implementors, applying innovation to grab onto a transient competitive edge or catch up to someone else's edge in their base businesses. Used in this way, innovation is principally a cost of sustaining market share rather than an investment to reorient a market, restructure a product category, or refocus a business.

Because it is so risky for megacorps to innovate, they get many of their new ideas from organizations that can innovate more easily. Large companies are idea adaptors. They observe their smaller competitors, see something they like, invest in it or acquire it, improve on it—in other words, adapt it to their own requirements—and then put their time and talent into executing or administering it.

Even when megacorps become concerned by the magnitude of their opportunity losses because of a lack of innovative profits, it is difficult for them to remedy the situation. General Foods is a case in point. Stuck for several years with earnings of less than $100 on every $1,000 of operating revenues, GF decentralized in the mid-1980s. It created three subsidiary corporations, one to grow grocery products, a second for processed meats, and a third for coffee. But each of these businesses was still a multibillion dollar megacorp in itself and remained much too unfocused, too cost-ridden and constrained by bureaucratic controls, and too inflexible to yield superior margins.

One of the reasons for creative constipation is that innovation needs redefinition in many megacorps. For most of them, it is traditional to make chief executive officers out of "lifers" who have spent their entire working careers at their companies, joining them at graduation and spending the next thirty years or so moving up the ranks. 3M does this all the time, even though it thinks of itself as a hotbed of innovation and change.

IBM sought remedy from similar problems in 1988 by decentralizing into five automonous organizations, each of which was given responsibility for its own product design, manufacturing, and marketing. It was hoped to give an innovative flourish to what a spokesperson for IBM described as "a fundamental change in the way we do our business." The restructured personal computer organization, as an example, was empowered to decide for itself when to bring out new models and what innovations they should contain that would not need to be justified to IBM headquarters. Top management would judge them only in the context of whether or not they met corporate financial and technological standards. Once he got approval, each business unit's general manager would have to blame his own product developers or marketers for being off plan. "Upstairs" would no longer be culpable.

IBM's reorganization was intended to solve one of a megacorp's most persistent problems—product development, or having the right product for the right market at the right time. For several years, IBM has had two growth models to choose from. The older of the two was called the "contention system" because it encouraged competing teams to pursue different prototypes of each new product. IBM's six-member management group would eventually hold a runoff and, after months or even years, a

winner would be appointed. By that time, competitors might have
entered the market first and the delay may have allowed them to
eat away at IBM's future market. Meanwhile, long after it had
demonstrated undeniable success, IBM's other growth model
remained in disuse. It was the remote, small, independent team
model that had produced the PC personal computer, created a
marketing channel for it, and became the Entry Systems Division
all within about a year.

It took until the 1990s for IBM to resurrect the "Dirty Dozen"
model that produced its PC so successfully a decade earlier.
When it rediscovered the formula, IBM used it to enter the laptop
computer business by putting together a small team that was
light on its feet and free. As a result, its laptops got to market in
fourteen months (equalling its rival, Toshiba) instead of the two-
to-three-year gestation time frame that is typical. To pull this off,
IBM relied on a handful of rules:

1. From the beginning, focus on what the customer wants.
2. Create small teams of no more than twenty people, about
   one-tenth the normal size.
3. Cut across traditional lines in assembling teams so that
   marketing and manufacturing can contribute to the product development process, and design and performance
   problems can be solved as they come up.
4. Let the developers build from other companies' parts.
5. Make it a commandment that once the specs are set, the
   specs are set.

Mixing Decentralization and Innovation

Decentralized autonomous business units empower their people,
freeing them to innovate. That is why megacorps are continually
looking for the most workable mix of centralized and decentralized operations. IBM likes to say that it never reorganizes except
for good business reasons. But if IBM has gone for a few years
without reorganizing, that in itself is considered to be a good
business reason.

Many megacorps that wait too long to restructure do it

wholesale. When Kodak was in its decision-making gridlock for a generation or more, products like color film that it had invented and whose markets it had dominated were overtaken one by one by competition. The few innovations Kodak made, such as the disk camera, failed. Then, in a single stroke, Kodak reorganized into twenty-four profit-centered business units.

General Electric worked for six years to make its businesses into a more wieldly mix. In the old way of doing things, each GE business head reported to a group head who reported to a sector head who reported to the chief executive officer. Each level had its own support staff in finance, marketing, and strategic planning. In the seventh year, all the groups and sectors were done away with and the business heads reported directly to the CEO, who had announced that he wanted to "open up the place so people can hit the home run."

Cincinnati Milacron has also decentralized, restructuring into five "focus factories" with one to manufacture each of its four major types of machines and the fifth for replacement parts. Each unit is responsible for its own product development.

McDonald's may offer another approach to innovation. Even though the company is a collection of individual entrepreneurs who are its franchisees, it employs a Vice President for Individuality whose job is to make the company "feel small." Johnson & Johnson tries to do the same thing by breaking its businesses into 166 autonomous companies.

No longer is money the main incentive to decentralize. Time is competitive advantage, the key to survival. Bringing a product to market slowly is very often the equivalent of failing to bring it to market at all. Time compression must be the goad of all megacorp operations. It is ancient history to say, as management at Deere & Co. has said, that "in our construction equipment division, it used to take five to seven years from when the idea for a product was first conceived to when the first machine came off the assembly like." In tomorrow's competition, the market opportunity window will long ago have been closed.

By the type of alliances and diversifications they make, megacorps reveal their competitive weaknesses. One of the ways that megacorps are attempting a perpetual renewal without innovation is through alliances with emergent growth companies.

Xerox, for example, invests in many independent high technology ventures. One of them is Kurzwell Applied Intelligence, a developer of voice recognition systems. Out of its total $22 million capitalization, $5 million of Kurzwell's funds represent investment by Xerox.

W. R. Grace has placed a $400,000 venture investment in Oral Research Laboratories to fund the development of a line of dental hygiene products. AT&T accounts for $4 million of American Telephone & Electronics Company's $40 million fund to manufacture wristwatch-based telephone message systems. General Electric is a prolific backer of computer systems, working from a venture fund of almost $300 million.

Coca-Cola, already a soft drink megacorp, is attempting to become a megacorp across several other industries by its "49 percent solution." This is Coke's way of describing the investment stakes of that size that it is funding in a diversity of businesses. The just-under-50 percent level of its investments allows Coke to maintain effective control yet enables the businesses it supports to access the equity markets as independent organizations. In addition, these businesses remain off Coke's books.

Coke is also applying its 49 percent formula to business ventures it already owns. It has sold to the public 51 percent of its bottling business. In the same way, McKesson has brought two of its business units public with a retained 49 percent ownership. US West and other Baby Bell companies are taking their cellular telephone businesses public the same way, keeping a minority investment.

Entering the 1990s, IBM had invested over half a billion dollars to obtain equity in software microcorps, turning itself into a general contractor of computer operating systems rather than a supplier of only its own homemade piece parts.

Sony Corporation went the other way. Instead of buying equity stakes in microcorps, Sony shares research know-how, makes production facilities available, and reveals business plans in partnering with complementary small companies. Sony looks to them to help expand the range of applications for Sony technologies. "We are good in video electronics," a Sony spokesperson says. "Panavision, Inc., is good in lens technology. If we make Panavision our ally, the two of us can accelerate the development of high-definition TV cameras. We will sell them, and Panavision will lease them. Both of us will grow."

When megacorps want to penetrate a new market without paying their up-front dues in seed time and money, another alternative is to reach out for someone else's business. Megabroker Shearson Lehman Hutton got into the business of investment counsel to early retirees by acquiring the niche operating group serving the retirement market at Dean Witter Reynolds. To provide the group with microcorp incentive, Shearson offered to pay its members 80 percent of the revenues they brought in for the first fourteen months. On top of that, the group would receive an additional 20 percent of the most lucrative two months' revenues.

In a similar way, megacorps are acquiring alternative distribution systems that can range from direct sales forces to third-party agents and nonpersonal selling systems like direct mail, mail order, and telemarketing. Relatedness in these cases is based more on the commonality of markets that are served than on specific types of service channels.

The conceptual basis for some agglomerations—just what constitutes "relatedness"—can be quite flexible. When Kodak bought Sterling Drug, it saw the union of the two megacorps as being complementary in two ways. Sterling has never had a strong R&D reputation; Kodak has. Kodak has never had a strong distribution system for its pharmaceutical products; Sterling has.

Acquisition of Sterling gave Kodak instant access to almost 900 sales representatives who sell prescription pharmaceuticals and over-the-counter products. This is a lot faster way for Kodak to get into the pharmaceutical business than screening 500,000 proprietary chemical compounds derived from the photography business to see if any of them has big-winner potential. But convenience has its price. The day after buying Sterling for over $5 billion in cash, Kodak's stock fell $4.25 a share. Sterling's share price rose $9.

Competing as a Microcorp

One of the most troublesome facts of life to megacorp managers is the unevenness of megacorp performance. No two divisions, departments, or lines of business deliver the same results. In reality, in spite of corporatewide cultures, megacorps hardly ever have a total unity about them. There really are no such entities as 3M, Kodak, or IBM in this sense.

Each of these companies has a small number of successes, a larger number of failures, and a mass of mediocrity in between. The same company can be pointed at to illustrate any of them. Extractive or industrial manufacturing companies that have consumer product divisions invariably make a mess of them. Technology-based companies that have consulting businesses generally run them into the ground. Mature companies that sponsor in-house business incubators most often suffocate their fledgling enterprises in their cribs. Megacorps are saved from the cross-pollination of their mistakes by the fact that most of their people do not talk to each other across functional lines. The downside of this blessing is that it also slows down the propagation of successes.

These facts of life open the door for a megacorp's smaller-size competitors. Some of them will want to become megacorps themselves by replicating the rates of growth of Compaq Computer, which made it in five years or Apple Computer, which took eight. Other competitors who are minicorp in size will combine in one fashion or another to become a real or de facto megacorp. The smallest competitors, the microcorps, will have a choice of three competitive strategies: They can obsolete a megacorp technology, niche a megacorp market, or become a megacorp's outsourced product development department.

In order to be competitive against megacorps, a microcorp must be successful because of its size rather than in spite of it. As a microcorp manager, you will have to:

- Hold a clear vision of your mission.
- Target a relatively narrow niche market for your vision.
- Produce customized products and services for your market.
- Specialize in applying your products to your customer businesses, embedding your products into comprehensive systems that contain equipment, installation, maintenance, training, and project management.
- Become the industry standard-bearer of the results.

A microcorp must generally compete on the basis of a technically innovative process or product in order to be able to grow its customers from a standing start. But it takes more than that. Microcorps must be the best appliers of their technology so that it makes a compelling difference to their customers' competitive viability. It is not just scientific knowledge that a micro requires, but also customer knowledge—how its users must put its technology to work and what added values will come of it when they do. Because microcorps must focus on a single customer constituency, they can afford to be caring organizations. In the expression of their care, they can be adaptively flexible and put forth a great deal of hustle.

Megacorps will find themselves at impossible disadvantages as they try to compete in fields where they have only a minor commitment against market specialists whose commitment is total. "Hind-tit" operations like 3M's consumer products division (an orphan in an otherwise industrial manufacturing company) and its polar opposite, Procter & Gamble's cellulose manufacturing operations (in an otherwise consumer products company), will have an increasingly difficult time going head to head with competitors who dedicate themselves completely to a single business. Even companies where the disparities are less, such as with AT&T's computer systems group in the bowels of an essentially telecommunications business, are finding it difficult to make a mark for themselves and convince customers that they are really serious and geared for the long haul.

In health care, specialty hospitals that devote themselves to a single illness or disease entity earn the highest profits. Among the most profitable specialties are psychiatric care, alcohol and drug abuse, physical rehabilitation, and Alzheimer's disease.

Among industrial businesses, Loctite is a prime example of microspecialization. Dozens of competitors, large and small, manufacture industrial adhesives. Nonetheless, Loctite commands a 100 percent price premium by targeting its Quick Metal brand to maintenance engineers who need to repair broken equipment fast until replacement parts arrive.

Another microcorp that dominates its niche is Patagonia, an outdoor clothing manufacturer. Its outerwear is made with unique features that are custom-tailored to its mountain-climbing market, such as breathable yet waterproof coatings, heavy-duty seams, multiple zippers for controlled ventilation, wide sleeve joints for easy lifting while climbing, and cutaway hood sections to ensure unimpeded peripheral vision.

Other successful microcorps are Porsche in high-technology automobiles, Cross Instruments in upscale writing supplies, Hyster in specialty forklift trucks, Ocean Spray in cranberry products, and Snap-On Tools, whose hand tools cost mechanics two and a half times more than their competition, but can be paid for over ten weeks without interest penalties. This understanding of how to help customers separates Snap-On from the "big guys" it competes against.

The success of microcorps such as these is due to two factors:

1. Because they do only one thing, they can do it exceedingly well. This gives them the benefits of *concentration*.
2. Because they serve a limited number of customers, they can be exceedingly flexible in applying what they make or market. This gives them the benefits of *customization*.

The combination of concentration and customization is hard to beat. It makes every customer special. He is the focus of the microcorp's entire business. His needs can be individualized in the ways they are cared for.

In order to maximize customer impact, microcorp managers are charged with creating a corporate culture that is dedicated to implementation. Because implementation can occur only inside a customer's business operations, microcorps must be skilled in auditing customer business functions, calculating their current contributions to costs or revenues, and then adding sufficient value to them to improve their contributions. Improving the contribution of a customer cost center means reducing its cost. For a profit center, improving its contribution means increasing its revenues and earnings.

Because implementation skills, not just technological wizardry, enable a mircrocorp to go beyond the development stage, Xomox has become a prototypical microcorp. Xomox has come to enjoy a de facto monopolistic profit structure in its business of manufacturing sleeve valves, a type of valve that has essentially the same basic form and concept today as valves made of lead that were found in the ruins of Pompeii in A.D. 79. This makes it something of an understatement to say that the slide valve industry is mature. Not only that, it is oversupplied by several hundred manufacturers. Yet Xomox has consistently earned a 30 percent average return on equity, the reward of the specialist.

The Xomox strategy is threefold: It concentrates, it customizes, and it adds a third value by consulting.

1. Xomox *concentrates* on manufacturing a single product, valves. As a marketer, it concentrates on selling them principally to the petrochemical industry.
2. Xomox *customizes* its valves to fit the specific chemical processes that can add or subtract the most significant values to petrochemical processors.
3. Xomox *consults* on the applications engineering of its valves and bases its prices, always set at a premium, on the dollar values it adds to each process by decreasing costs or improving productivity. Xomox is paid for the values it adds, not the valves it sells. Each value is the result of an amalgam: valves, applications engineering services, and customer training.

The core value of Xomox consultation is its store of knowledge of how to make petrochemical processors more competitive. Xomox knows where their major costs cluster, by how much it can reduce them, and what the dollar values of the reduced costs can amount to. It also knows where productivity can be improved, by how much it can improve output, and what the dollar values of the improved output—and its effect on sales—can be at each stage of the customer life cycle.

As the industry standard in petrochemicals processing, Xomox knows more about how to apply valve technology to reduce costs and increase productivity than its customers know or its competitors have learned. That is one half of the equation of its specialist positioning. The other half is that Xomox knows more about how to translate its applications into new customer profits than either its customers or competitors can achieve without it.

Xomox wins against megacorps because it is an *applier* of valves instead of merely a *supplier* of them.

Competing as a Minicorp

If you are a minicorp, larger than a microcorp but still a relatively small competitor against megaworld standards, you will be an endangered species in tomorrow's competition. From below, you will be niched to death by the microcorps in your industry; from above, you will find yourself too close to the cost structure and productivity of megacorps to have any competitive advantage yet too top-heavy and diverse to parallel the cost-effective focus and flexibility of microcorps.

Minicorps will be at mortal risk every minute of their lives, either from doing themselves in or from being done in by a shifting of their market niche, a leapfrogging of their technology, or a price cutting by a larger competitor of their key cash cow.

The middle ground is disappearing everywhere. In computer retailing, Ed Anderson, president of Computerland, discovered that "You have to make a choice: Either go the superstore route or to a much smaller operation. . . . If you stay in the middle, you're going to die."

Management at Unisys, a midsize producer in the computer industry, has expressed the minicorp paradox as a choice: "Computer companies can go two ways. They can attempt to become full-service, international players or they can become subsuppliers to the big guys. The middle ground—$500 million to perhaps $10 billion in sales—is increasingly untenable."

Data General is another computer company that wanted to play in the big leagues with the two computer megacorps, IBM and Digital Equipment Corporation. But within a few years, Data General's plans to expand into several new markets were called "strategic errors" by its chairman, Edson de Castro. He found himself unable to make the passage from minicorp to megacorp. Finding himself caught while in transit, he concluded that "large companies really aren't comfortable doing business with companies our size"—too small to be a comprehensive systems supplier but too big to be a niche player. Because most megacorp customers are at greater ease with fellow megasuppliers, Data General has had to refocus on smaller, minicorp-type customers who are more in its own league. This restructuring of its vision has led to a restructuring of its organization, operations, body count, and product lines and the dismissal of its top management.

From having "dispersed too much organizationally and geographically" as well as diversified too broadly into too many products and markets, Data General is on the leading edge of solving one of tomorrow's central problems: how to be profitable yet remain a mid-size competitor in the megaworld.

Litton Industries has tried many of the same remedies. Litton has moved out of business computers and calculators, medical products, and office furniture where it was unlikely to be more than an also-ran minicorp and has consolidated in three businesses where it believes that it can be a major player: oil services, defense electronics, and industrial automation. With this strategy, Litton is also following the model of General Electric. At GE, cost cutting is allowed to go on for a while in order to improve margins in a micro or mini business that does not grow or a megabusiness that is no longer growing. But as soon as GE determines that a business is not good enough to be number 1 or no longer a growth business, GE divests it.

A minicorp's competitiveness tomorrow will depend on one of two strategies: Either it must ally with megacorps or ally against them. Either way, the keystone to competitiveness will be alliance. By allying with one or more megacorps, a minicorp will become a captive supplier. By allying against them with other minicorps, it may be able to create a critical mass that can equalize the megacorp advantage.

In every industry, minicorps are coming together defensively to provide more formidable competition for their industry megacorps. Banking is an example, where the money-center giants have been broadening their base from major metropolitan areas into parts of the country that are the historical preserve of medium- and smaller-size regional banks. To compete against the megabanks, two and sometimes three interstate minibanks are merging into a single superregional bank. The objective is to control up to 80 percent of the assets in their regions.

In Europe, spurred on by the Common Market, minicorps

are partnering with other companies of their same size across
formerly sacrosanct national borders. They are choosing to relinquish some of their nationalism for the sake of stronger research
and development, economies of scale, extended marketing capabilities, and cost savings from the elimination of duplicate product
lines and processes.

Sweden's minicorp ASEA and the minicorp BBC Brown Boveri of Switzerland have become an electrical equipment megacorp
that makes products for the entire continental market. They
manage their combined business in the "American style" with
emphasis on profits and use English as their common language.

The track record of minicorp partnerships has been fraught
with problems that have shown themselves to be sticky, expensive, and difficult to cope with. Unisys, the partnering of minicorps Burroughs and Univac, has never succeeded in becoming
one company. Yet it has tried to grow to megacorp stature by
adding more partners in the belief that "size will ensure success."
Unisys acquired Timeplex, a maker of multiplexers for transmit-
ting computer data, and Convergent Technologies, a niche-mar-
keting manufacturer of desktop computers. The goal was to turn
Unisys into a $20 billion company by 1993. But by 1989, Unisys
was facing flat mainframe sales, excess inventory, cost overruns,
and top management defections at both Timeplex and Convergent.

Minicorps take their problems with them when they merge
into a megabusiness. Uniroyal and B. F. Goodrich became the
second-largest American tire producer when they formed Uniroyal Goodrich Tire Company in 1986. Their merger was followed
by the shutdown of two of the company's nine factories, the
layoff of 1,200 employees, and a staggering financial burden from
their combined debt and pension obligations. Animosity pre-
vailed between the Uniroyal people and the Goodrich people,
along with confusion. For a long while, there were two sets of
everything—accountants, engineering forces, and information
management systems—that were completely different and incompatible.

When Chevron and Gulf merged in 1984, they had "four
years of turmoil—turmoil for the employees, turmoil for everybody." In the process of absorbing Gulf, Chevron had to sell

billions of dollars worth of assets and reduce the combined work force by 25,000 while being "diverted from doing things we might otherwise have been doing."

Yet going it alone can be disastrous. Tomorrow's minicorp managers will have to learn how to live with other minicorps. Minicorps have many natural affinities. To make them pay off they need to accelerate each other's ability to make their combined customers more competitive. Complementary and supplementary resources must be seamlessly pooled. Duplicate resources must be reallocated or divested. In the final analysis, it will take the "third partner," the customer, to catalyze his minicorp partners in his own best interests as well as theirs.

As a result of tomorrow's new corporate structures and economic stringencies, minicorps must learn how to ally their assets—especially their capabilities to act as applications experts for their customers—or they will be squeezed out of their markets from above and below. Megacorps must learn how to "deglomerate" their bureaucracies to free up managerial autonomy to innovate everything they make and do. Microcorps that want to remain independent must learn how to accelerate their growth at a faster rate than ever before if they are going to avoid getting bogged down as burned-out minicorps or swept up by the gravity fields of megacorps that see them as a substitute for innovation.

II

Tomorrow's Winning Strategies

3

Competitive Re-Visioning

Tomorrow's competitiveness will be absolute. Whereas yesterday a business could be relatively competitive and survive, even prosper, in tomorrow's competition a business will have to be number 1 or a close number 2 in its field or it will be noncompetitive. If you end up as a number 3, no one will want to partner with you. You will have to go it alone or, perhaps even worse, partner with another number 3 business that has also found itself without a chair when the music stopped in its own industry.

Being number 1 or number 2 does not mean that you must be a Fortune 500 company. It means that you must be your industry's standard-bearer of customer value or its runner-up. It means that you must share the ambition of top managers like W. R. Grace's president J. P. Bolduc, who has said, "I don't want to be in businesses in which I'm the tail; I want to be in businesses in which I'm the dog—the top dog." The day when every dog could have its day was yesterday.

Number 3 companies will fall back into the second tier of suppliers, the outer ring of also-rans. They will do the bulk of their business as subcontractors to the number 1 and 2 companies in their industries rather than deal directly with their traditional customers. The number 1 and 2 companies will be known as strategic suppliers, dedicated allies of major customers who integrate multivendor systems and manage many of their customers' facilities and business categories as long-term partners. The number 3 companies will be their anonymous sources.

In the second tier, companies will be at continual risk of being consumed by merger and acquisition. Others will cycle through periodic downsizings, selling off or writing off assets that are no longer competitive and retreating under hot pursuit into their core capabilities. If they cannot discover an uncommon expertise, many will simply vanish.

Tomorrow's vision of competitiveness is different from yesterday's. It still emphasizes a growing rate of profit accumulation, still positions businesses for market leadership and makes customer satisfaction the prime objective. But no definition of tomorrow's competitiveness will be meaningful unless it mandates a *compelling reason* for your company's customers to buy from you. This is the steak. Everything else is parsley.

Every move your business makes must be dedicated to creating, validating, and perpetuating the reasons why customers must do business with you. Every strategy must pass the "compelling reason" test: If we do this, does it enhance our market's compulsion to buy from us? When the answer is no, the strategy must become automatically null.

If you lose your vision in terms of its compelling reason, you may lose your market. This is what happened to Control Data Corporation, one of the foremost makers of scientific computers from the early 1960s through the late 1970s. By 1980 the company had lost its way. It began to deemphasize its computer systems in favor of computer-based services that were supposed to address "society's current needs." By 1986 CDC's share of the large-scale computer market had fallen to less than 3 percent. There turned out to be no compensating market for serving society's current needs.

A new manager who took over CDC's Computer Systems Group said that, as a result of fogged vision, "we didn't know where our machines were, what they were being used for, where the market was going, and where we fit into it." Control Data was being called Out-of-Control Data.

What will the competitors of tomorrow look like? Will they resemble Timken, which regularly takes losses to maintain volume by accepting prices on its products that are far below their value? Will they be like Black & Decker, which has a policy of meeting competitive prices no matter how low? Will they be like 3M's Electronics & Information Technologies business, which invests millions of dollars in building brand loyalty by giving away its products at cut rates? Instead of trading off margins for volume, will tomorrow's competitors be like Chaporral Steel in eliminating almost all its staff positions and making its line managers act as their own customer service representatives? Or will they be like General Electric, whose product groups are being narrowed down to a "focused few" fourteen businesses with the objective to be number 1 or 2 in each of them or get out?

Changing the Critical Factors of Success

From now on, each year will present its own changing challenge. Who will lead the world: the United States, Japan, Germany, or the larger European Community? Japan has money, technological prowess, and a focused, homogeneous people. So, to a lesser extent, does Germany. As Europe's market becomes increasingly unified, it may be able to exceed even the United States in the size of its gross community product. Yet Alfred Herrhausen as chairman of Deutsche Bank said about the United States, "If you decide to be the world leader, and act like it, you will be." The Japanese government's adviser Seizaburo Sata sees it the same way: "The twentieth century was the American century. And the twenty-first century will be the American century."

At the corporate level as well as internationally, leadership will not simply be based on mass, money, or market size. Leadership, the power that enables a business to be the maximum contributor to its customers' competitive advantage, will come from a new combination of critical success factors.

Tomorrow's competitors have to be better envisioners of growth. They have to get the future right the first time, acting more like Joseph Wilson of Xerox than Thomas Watson of IBM in recognizing the next xerography, and more like Thomas Watson than Ralph Cordiner of GE in recognizing the next revolution in data processing, and more like Ralph Cordiner than Gwilyn Price of Westinghouse to gear up to invest in the right future of household electrical appliances.

Tomorrow's competitors have to be better commercializers of invention. They have to be more like Will Durant of General Motors than J. P. Morgan in building businesses around the next automobile, and more like Henry Ford than Will Durant in recognizing that more cars could be marketed as replacements for horses than as competitors of trolley cars and railroads, and more like Alfred Sloan of GM than Henry Ford in seeing that the mass sale of cars was more dependent on widely available consumer credit than on mass manufacturing.

Tomorrow's competitors have to be smarter market segmenters than their predecessors at B. F. Goodrich, who believed that "the best way to run a tire company is to make as many tires as possible," and their fellow believers at the old U.S. Steel Company, to whom it was gospel that "when we make the tonnage we make the dollars," or at Exxon, where gallonage was the equivalent of tonnage, or at Du Pont, where yardage was the equivalent of gallonage.

Tomorrow's competitors have to be better business positioners than Unisys, whose managers thought of themselves as being in the same big league as IBM and Digital Equipment Corporation. As a result, they geared up to be a full-time supplier and ended up with many of their lines competing in the minor leagues. Tomorrow's competitors will also have to be better at competing on value than the Univac division of Unisys, where the shipment of 40,000 highly discounted computers one year earned only the same amount of revenue as 25,000 units shipped the year before.

Unlike past generations, when access to low-cost capital, low labor rates, and the economies that can come from large scale were success factors for competitiveness, no major competitor or alliance will be constrained by shortages of cash or distribution channels. Nor will any company be able to have a headlock for long on technology, which is being uniformly replicated all over the world. Every technology will be a threat and a resource to every other technology. The deciding factor in competitiveness will be the right vision of where technology and markets are headed so that you can position yourself at their most likely intersections in advance of the crowd.

It will be more important to own markets than technologies, although ownership of technologies will be periodically crucial, when they are new, to starting out as the dominant player in a market. Losing a market, or failing to capture a significant share of it, will hurt more than the immediate loss of business. No matter how scientifically out in front you may be, forfeiting a major market will be followed by losing out on growing the technology. Without daily applications experience and imersion in the user values that determine customer satisfaction, there will be no way to maintain market leadership. Once this is gone, the next evolution of technology may go along with it because each migration rides the coattails of knowledge of its predecessor.

The Japanese strategy of investing continuously in "the next generation," always looking for breakthroughs into new businesses, will have to become everybody's strategy. Many companies have the traditional habit pattern of doing the opposite by walking away from the risk and expense of what comes next. At General Electric, for example, the R&D philosophy has been that "a new appliance for our major appliance division is more important than a new game." In tomorrow's competition, this kind of game risks becoming an endgame.

Companies that are unable to market their technologies will have to try turning around their battleships in bathtubs in order to face, and face up to, their demand sources. Tektronix, Inc., and Hewlett-Packard Company are similar technology-driven electronics businesses that serve several similar markets. Both have believed in letting their engineers do whatever they wanted, from designing their own ergonomic chairs at Tektronix to chasing after virtually any business that they could build a product for at HP. Neither company has had a market-driven strategy that puts customer competitiveness first. One of Tek's several successive presidents in the late 1980s, David Friedley, spoke for both companies when he said that most of his "whiz-bang people wouldn't know a customer if they saw one."

Sorting Out the Winners and Also-Rans

In the last quarter of the twentieth century, the entry requirements for competitiveness have gone steadily up. By now, flattening out the corporate hierarchy, pushing authority all the way down the organization to speed up decisions, getting closer to the customer, realizing that small is beautiful and that you bring focus to a business when you create a stand-alone, autonomous operation that runs on entrepreneurial principles and practices are Christmasses past. Any business that needs to learn them for the first time today or feels proud to proclaim them tomorrow will be lost in the shuffle, swept away by newer realities.

Tomorrow's competition is all about maximizing value, both your own and your customers'. In order to maximize your value, you will have to concentrate on each market you serve as if it were your one and only market—the benign myth of "the sole customer"—so that you can dominate its standards for value. You will have to imbue your entire organization with customer values, starting with research and development where your customers' needs must be represented so that they are always "alive and well" there. You must couple your R&D with engineering and manufacturing and then correlate them with your marketing so that the manufactured values you build in are the values that your customers need.

Every company has trouble coordinating their engineers and marketers. Yet no company can afford to let this continue. As Robert Cizik, chief executive of Cooper Industries Inc., has observed with his own marketers, "They walk down to the manufacturing people and say, 'Now manufacture it.' " The manufacturers return the compliment later when they walk back up to the marketers and say, "Now sell it." Each walks away unpartnered, giving no thought to the other's capabilities. The customer gets caught in between. Nothing will change until the marketers no longer have to "walk down" to manufacturing or the manufacturers have to walk back up, because they will be organizationally teamed together with their common master, their customer, who will enforce market values on them both.

Because your customers' values must dominate your vision,

you must get used to seeing yourself as an applications-oriented, applications-dedicated, and applications-sophisticated business because that is where the values will be for your customers and, as a result, that is where the profits will be for you. You must sell applications values the only way their benefits can be maximized for you and your customers and that is in a consultative, non-vending manner. And everywhere you want to be the counsel of choice on competitive advantage for your customers, you will have to get there first or find yourself number 2 to a competitor who does.

Champion managers have a vision of their enterprises that is built around a portrait of their customers. Tom Carvel, a Greek immigrant who put together a chain of 700 ice cream stores starting with a $15 loan from his future wife, insisted on acting as his own corporate spokesman in radio and television commercials in spite of a raspy, gravelly voice and disabled diction. "The professionals ridicule my commercials," he acknowledged. "You can have a six-foot-tall, handsome announcer with a perfect voice, perfect diction, perfect grammar. But very few ice cream buyers look like that. Our commercials are for the people who look like us, talk like us, and sound like us."

The supercritical success factors that drive tomorrow's competitiveness will reward you if you have done your homework on the 1980s and, conversely, they will severely penalize you if you used the 1980s just to pull even with the 1970s. In tomorrow's competition, there will be no Big Eights or Big Sixes and few Big Threes.

The horizontal growth strategy of the past, which enabled companies to become for a time self-sustaining conglomerates chock-full of mature, commodity-type businesses, has given way to a market-centered segmentation where everybody does only what he does best—that is, only things that make capital rather than tie it up. The old-style General Motorization and Procter & Gambleization of businesses with everything under one roof will be artifacts of the past, unaffordable and unmanageable for maximum returns on the maximum investments they require.

In the 1840s, the basic business of Procter & Gamble was soap. When P&G discovered edible tallow in soap fats, it became a manufacturer and marketer of low-margin cottonseed oil. In order to protect its asset base by pricing up the barriers to entry, P&G built thirty cottonseed crushing mills. As cottonseed oil became a high-volume commodity, P&G decided to extract the cellulose from it and sell it as a low-margin ingredient for viscose rayon production. In order to meet the demand for more cellulose than could be extracted from its cottonseed oil, P&G purchased pine forests in Florida. When supply exceeded demand and the cellulose mill had idle time, P&G filled it by producing paper pulp. Exactly 122 years after P&G began marketing cottonseed oil to begin this chain of asset-incurring events, the company finally found a use for the mill's paper pulp in disposable diapers.

No company will be able to afford to grow like this again. There are too many others things to do with impatient capital and, at any given time, not enough capital to do them with. The asset collectors of the past, waiting patiently for an unknown future to come along, will disappear.

Tomorrow's competitors—the successful ones—will have to learn the two secrets that determine future competitiveness: Add value to the competitive advantage of high-growth customers so they add competitive advantage to you, and add only the minimal assets to your own business that enable you to do so.

Re-Visioning "Our Game"

When customer competitiveness becomes the drive force for your corporate vision, you can compile a vision grid along the lines of the model shown in Figure 1. The grid allows you to correlate a customer's compelling needs for competitive advantage with your corporate capability to serve him. Where they both match up on the high side, you will come upon your version of "Our Game," the solution to customer growth challenges in which you have the best chance to become your customers' industry standard. Adjoining your Game will be the high-to-medium matchups where you may have diversification opportunities into logically extended solutions.

If you have a high capability where a customer has only a medium need for competitive advantage, you may be taking on a problem of overcapacity or overengineering a product. In that

Figure 1. Vision grid.

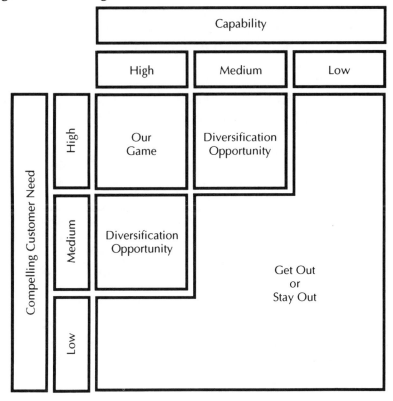

case, you should look for another customer. If you have a medium capability where a customer has a high need, you may be asking to be a number 3 source. Unless you can upgrade your cost-effectiveness and become the industry standard, you can probably allocate your resources elsewhere more successfully.

The Vision Grid (Figure 1) warns you to get out or stay out of businesses where your capability to compel customers to do business with you is low and customer compulsion to buy from you is also low. If Anheuser-Busch had used the Vision Grid, it might not have gotten off-line in its penetrations of the food business. Conversely, Combustion Engineering was able to envision a successful move up the value chain from its core capability of facility construction to the far more profitable and customer-partnering capability of facility management.

"Our Game" shows you your clearest shots at advantaging your customers where you have the opportunity to win a number 1 position. Unless you have such a capability, you will only be an also-ran or out of the running altogether. The businesses that your clear shots give you will be your core moneymakers. On their peripheries you may find diverse chances to stretch your cores or innovate in areas where new cores can be created. These will be questionable shots, not clear ones. But the warning that they should be approached with caution does not mean that they should not be approached.

If you cannot elevate your capability from medium to high, or if you cannot do it cost-effectively, you may want to consider forming a strategic alliance with another supplier. You should look for a partner who has an underutilized high capability or can put such a capability together jointly with you. A small company with a leading-edge technology or, if you are a mid-size company, another medium-level business, could be appropriate partner material.

The Vision Grid is a summary statement of your strategic business plan. It pinpoints your growth capabilities, your growth markets, and your next-generation growth opportunities. When you assign dollar values to each of them, both for yourself and your customers, you will know exactly where you stand as one of tomorrow's competitors.

Squinting Through a Blurred Vision

Competitiveness is transient. Advantage is fleeting and perishable. It can fall away from any company, of any size, at any time, if a company loses the vision of its compelling reason for being in business and the customers who are compelled to do business with it. Small companies like Computer Memories, Inc., are especially vulnerable. Their visions blur easily from being undercapitalized, unsure of themselves or their mission, and unable to resist what can look like a sure thing even though it may go against their original dream. For its first two years of life, CMI's computer disk drive business boomed. It had several major customers and sales were going along at the $120 million level. Its stock was trading at $32. Then its managers abandoned their vision of CMI as a high-growth, stand-alone company and succumbed to becoming IBM's exclusive supplier. Within a year, IBM dropped CMI. It was reduced to a holding company shell with three employees and a stock value of $1.80.

Large companies take longer to lose their competitiveness when their visions blur. But when this happens, how large a business may be or even the fact that it once invented its industry and owned its markets is immaterial.

Kodak is an example of a company that has lost its competitive edge in the industry it not only created but controlled for almost 100 years. In the yearly 1970s, Kodak owned a virtual monopoly in the American market for color-negative film. By the middle 1980s, its share had shrunk by 20 percent. Once the acknowledged technology leader, both in film and in many types of cameras, in 1986 Kodak was at best a distant second to Fuji and often third or worse. Kodak had lost its customer focus. Engineer-managed, product- and process-driven, almost exclusively promoting its managers from within, and percolating even minor decisions all the way to the top, Kodak lost its sight-line to its markets. When that became apparent, Kodak managers tried diversification by buying entrepreneurial high-technology companies that were leaders in their fields. One by one, each of them lost its vision, then its competitiveness.

Since the 1970s, a small group of Kodak managers has been keeping an eye on a rival science, electronic imaging, that uses filmless cameras to record pictures on computerized disks for display through television screens. But electronic technology has always been a divisive issue at Kodak, being seen as not-invented-here and therefore a threat to the traditional film business.

By 1990 a dozen companies had already become superior to Kodak in electronic hardware, among them Sony and Matsushita, whose visions of the new-age customer are clearer because they have no historical ties to film and paper photography. At that time, Kodak took what it regarded as "a definitive stand" by targeting its objective to be "the world's best in both electronic and traditional imaging." In spite of throwing money at the problem—one quarter of Kodak's $1.3 billion annual R&D budget—it will be well past the year 2000, if then, before electronic imaging can make a major contribution to Kodak's business. By then, Kodak may be second, third, or worse among its competitors in each of its major industries.

In the meantime, Kodak's funds for electronic imaging will have to come from reallocating resources while still trying to grow its other core businesses of information systems, chemicals, and pharmaceuticals. To feed all of them and subsidize electronic imaging at the same time is a herculean task. Kodak now sees the problem if not the solution: "To protect the long-range viability of our photography business, we've got to get into electronic imaging. The question is how to do that in a way that creates value and doesn't consume all your resources. That's the challenge." It is compounded by management's vision of the company's current mix of businesses, which it expresses as being "enamored with all of them."

Similar losses of competitive vision have occurred to RCA, Union Carbide, International Harvester, TWA, and Pan Am. Some change their names, some merge or are acquired, others restructure and downsize. All lose competitiveness and, with it, tomorrow's profits, markets, and leadership.

How does a once-competitive business fall from competitiveness? Why does a new business fail to ever become competitive?

The reasons that are usually put forward are cutthroat foreign competition from government-subsidized players, the changing value of the dollar, restrictive union work rules and wage scales, obsolete government regulations, industry maturity, and market apprehensions or misapprehensions. Some or all of these causes are invariably operative. They distort the playing field, making it less than level. But one reason for noncompetitiveness almost always prevails: *A business loses its competitiveness because it does not have a compelling vision of how to make its customers more competitive.*

Adopting an Unconventional Look

Noncompetitiveness tomorrow is guaranteed by practicing today's conventional wisdom. Conventional wisdom in managing a business produces only conventional profits. Sameness in competitive strategy only produces parity in market position based on sameness of products, pricing, and promotion.

It is not that conventional wisdom is wrong. After all, it has become conventional by accumulating over the ages, tested by time. But because it is conventional, it is expected; because it is expected, it can easily be defended against, either countered or neutralized. It fails the definition of strategy, which means being unconventional.

When strategy becomes "doing what comes naturally" in an industry, it forsakes the crucial element of surprise. The more predictable a business allows itself to become, the easier it is for its competitors to defend against it and for its customers to dismiss it. Turning an industry on its ear is rarely possible or necessary for the average competitor. But tilting your approach as little as one degree from the commonplace is always possible and often represents the difference between being compelling and being lost in the crowd.

Conventionally applied, conventional wisdom leads to look-alike, think-alike, and act-alike competitors who could exchange strategic plans without incurring either undue risk or reward and who prove it by the free and easy way they interchange market shares, key customers, and middle and top-level managers. Their product lines are homogenized into me-too commodities, their mission statements read like photocopies, and their markets play them off one against the other in the hopes of discovering some compelling reasons to do business with them.

A company's "vision statement" gives the tip-off on the degree of its farsightedness—i.e., the extent to which the company envisions its customers first, or conventional nearsightedness. Farsighted visions dedicate a business to enhancing its customers' competitive advantage. Nearsighted visions still search for excellence by establishing a culture that promotes quality work, prevents defects, eliminates waste, and gives all products and services superior quality.

This kind of nearsighted vision is introspectively focused on a company's own bellybutton. It predisposes a business to issue conventional Statements of Business Purpose or Mission Statements that dedicate a business to "provide high-quality products, services, and systems" rather than high-quality profits and competitive advantage for the customers of its products, services, and systems:

- ○ It is conventional for a business to focus on growing itself. It is *unconventional* for a business to grow itself by first growing its customers.
- ○ It is conventional for a business to sell its products based on their features and benefits. It is *unconventional* for a business to sell its products' contributions to customer profits.
- ○ It is conventional for a business to base its prices on costs and competition. It is *unconventional* for a business to base its prices on the value of new profits it adds to its customers' bottom lines.
- ○ It is conventional for a business to seek the largest share of the largest market. It is *unconventional* for a business to maximize profits rather than market share and to prefer to market to specialized vertical niches rather than wholesale mass markets.
- ○ It is conventional for a business to make complete product lines in order to dominate distribution. It is *unconventional* for a business to make strategic alliances with suppliers of complementary products in order to market them together without having to manufacture all of them in-house.
- ○ It is conventional for a business to be organized around its basic processes. It is *unconventional* for a business to organize divisionally around each of its major markets.

Using traditional business thinking, companies commonly put the cart before the horse. They do what 3M does: "Someone comes up with a product and we try learning something about the market." Most of the time, this conventional approach to product development teaches its practitioners that there is no market, or at least no profitable market. Too late, they already have sunk costs into materials technology, product engineering, and manufacturing. Conventional wisdom says that there is nothing wrong with such random development. "It takes a couple of thousand random tries to get one good hit" with this method at 3M.

Meanwhile, unconventional managers who are weary of kissing thousands of frogs to find a single prince wonder what would happen if the 3M approach were to be reversed so that "someone comes up with a market and we try learning something about its needs."

It is conventional for a business to follow the conventional wisdom. When it does not, when it defies convention and acts unconventionally, it distinguishes itself from its competitors. Instead of courting similarity with competition and being an adversary with customers, an unconventional business can turn these relationships around.

Conventional wisdom has always obscured a business's vision of its customers. When David Sarnoff envisioned the future competitiveness of radio in the early 1900s, he tried to interest Eldridge Johnson in it because Johnson was already conversant with sound transmission as president of the Victor Talking Machine Company. But, to Johnson, radio was unconventional compared to the phonograph. When Sarnoff had finally made his money from radio, he paid convention the supreme compliment. He bought out Johnson and operated Victor as a division of RCA.

Planning Against the New-Age Difficulties

Tomorrow's competition puts a quickened emphasis on gaining the type of competitive advantage that comes from separating a single business or alliance out of its jell of congealed sharers of a common market. This will present difficulties to practitioners who still cling to outmoded visions of their businesses:

• It will be difficult for process-driven companies modeled along the lines of 3M to go on developing materials without markets for them and then waving them aloft to see if they can attract a bidder with a need.

• It will be difficult for hierarchy-driven companies modeled along the lines of Kodak to go on percolating decisions upward while opportunity windows close, costs escalate, and competitors are ready beginning to take ownership of a market.

• It will be difficult for technology-driven companies modeled along the lines of Hewlett-Packard to go on funding R&D more heavily than sales in the belief that performance superiority in their products is the source of profit superiority in their markets.

• It will be difficult for plant-driven companies modeled along the lines of Du Pont to go on equating their value with what goes into their products while paying less attention to their customers' sense of value based on what comes out.

• It will be difficult for multiproduct-driven companies modeled along the lines of General Electric to go on producing full lines that contain something for everybody and inviting niche marketers to "cherrypick" them by focusing on the 20 percent of products in a market that account for 80 percent of profits.

• It will be difficult for metal-bending businesses that make hardware of any kind, whether computers or catheters or compressors, to prevent their annual performance gains from outpacing their ability to price them commensurately. It will be even more difficult if such businesses remain so driven by their performance specifications that they compete on the basis of who has this year's "hottest box."

• It will be difficult for companies that relate the concept of service solely to their products and cannot fulfill the newly escalated demands for service in terms of application, implementation, information, education, and consultation rather than simply replacement and repair.

• It will be difficult for all companies to compete tomorrow if they maintain themselves as cultural culs-de-sac, promoting only from within, requiring that all new hires be engineers or chemists or any other speciality, and keeping glass ceilings over assertive women and aggressive minority groups. It will be even more difficult if their ombudsmen focus only on smoothing dissent and occasionally roiling attitudinal complacency and behavioral uniformity.

The evolutionary cycle of product-based businesses into "noncreative obsolescence" will intensify in tomorrow's competition as products, no matter how high their original technology may be, become commodities at an accelerated rate and lose their ability to command the premium margins they could enjoy when they were still branded.

As Figure 2 shows, sellers of technology-based products will be "low men on the totem pole" of unit margins if all they have to sell is their technology. They can take temporary refuge in upgrading their offerings to put applications-based services out in front of their products so that their businesses become repositioned as service suppliers with product support. But the safest harbor for margin insurance will be managing customer facilities instead of selling products or services to them. The ability to manage a customer's operation represents the true culmination of a supplier's expertise in knowing how to apply his own

Figure 2. Margin insurance path.

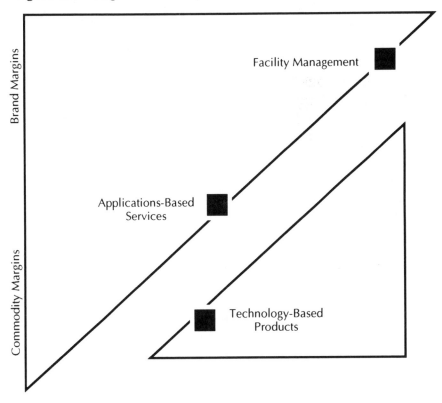

business to the businesses of his customers. It therefore deserves to be well compensated. It will command a combination of the highest fees and the lowest costs of sales since products and services will be bundled under a management contract without having to be individually sold on their merits.

Reversing Established Values

In a universe of replicated management styles, stereotypical plans and policies, and predictably repetitive strategies, it is brave to dare deviation in how a business is "seen." Where everyone sees price and quality as directly proportional—after all, you get what you pay for—competitive advantage goes to the defiance of convention that unites low price with high quality. Where everyone sees a value in controlled obsolescence over time—after all, never change a winning game; why fix it if it "ain't broke"?—competitive advantage goes to the defiance of convention that compresses evolutionary change in a single quantum leap. Where everyone sees that products must be sold hard on their features and benefits—after all, what do customers buy?—competitive advantage goes to the defiance of convention that sells a product's contribution to customer competitiveness rather than justifying its contribution to customer cost.

Turbulence in an industry or discontinuity in a market is an invitation to opportunity. If it does not come about naturally, it must be created. When convention is disrupted and the old order is in disarray, a market is up for grabs. Who can restructure it? To envision it anew means to play a controlling role in its future. The same holds true for unconventional management. It can act as a controlling influence, unsettling its players from carrying out cookie-cutter strategies, distracting them from the mechanical execution of boilerplate plans, and making them tentative about trendy thinking. Unconventional management is, in sum, competitive. For that reason, it will have to be the management style of tomorrow.

Leaders have often waited to see which way their followers were going before they took leadership. The leaders had oversight but no vision. It has been difficult for many of them to learn that one has to (1) be willing to bet the business on a vision and (2) be able to get one's people to buy into it. That is the only way growth comes about.

In virtually every major industry throughout business history, one company has envisioned a way to make its customers more competitive while others ignored what it was doing and went about the mutually destructive business of competing against each other. The lesson of competitiveness went unheeded: *Compete against the costs and competitors of your customers, not your own rival suppliers, and you will be compelling.*

According to yesterday's values, a dollar taken from a competitive supplier is more highly valued than a dollar of cost rescued for a customer or a dollar of new revenues earned for him. An improved product is more highly valued than the improvement it can make in a customer process. Tomorrow, these values will be reversed. Companies that compete first and foremost against the costs and competitors of their customers will have focused on the vision of tomorrow.

If you run your business with tomorrow's vision, you make quality products with what Detroit calls "good fit and finish," but you do not sell the products; you sell their value to your customers. You provide product-related services but you do not apply them only to your products; you apply them to improving the customer operations where your products are installed and implemented. You maintain sales forces but they do not vend products; they consult in the improvement of their customers' profits. You charge premium prices in return for premium value but you do not assess them as prices; you convert them to investments and correlate them with their return. You develop markets but you never deal with your major accounts as customers; you partner them and commit to grow their businesses jointly. You manufacture your biggest profit winners but eschew full lines; you ally yourself to other manufacturers who round out your lines to free you from the costs of rounding.

Reversing the way that the role of technology is seen in tomorrow's competition will be a necessary part of your competitive vision. Technology will be implicit in every aspect of competition, whether it is based on new combinations of molecules that produce advanced materials or interactive computer-driven information systems that connect marketing and manufacturing in real time. Yet there will be no competitive advantage in technology itself because all competitors will have equal access to its highest, most commercializable states of art. Technologies will be standardized at universally acceptable levels to the point where, like the products that come out of them, they become commodity resources. There will be no limits on putting them to work. Nor will there be any inherent advantage in doing so. The advantage will come from superior strategy in their application, implementation, and execution to grow your customer base.

Who can apply technology to be the best integrator of market research with product design, for example? Who can best interconnect design with manufacturing? Who can make it possible to serve increasingly finite market segments more flexibly so that profits can be made on small, highly customized product runs? Who can best understand that science and customer knowledge must be welded together so that the product development process and the customer satisfaction process become one and the same? Who can restructure the basic business organization framework to ensure that customer requirements are inextricably linked to technical capabilities so that the products that come out of R&D reflect the customer more than the inventor?

Unless technology is organized as a part of the value-creation process and is not regarded as a creator of value itself, it will not provide much in the way of competitive advantage.

Putting Customer Competitiveness First

Each of your businesses must achieve its own competitiveness. If a business is to do so strategically—that is, by virtue of its own planning and execution—it must compete by showing its markets that it is worth more than the values they can add to their own businesses independently or in partnership with any other supplier. *To be competitive, you must be seen as more valuable.*

This says that you must not seek your competitiveness by either of two means, both of which circumvent value. One is price. Competitiveness cannot be bought. To be cheaper is not to be more valuable. Indeed, potential customers may infer that the value is commensurate with its price and is therefore less.

Neither can competitiveness be gained by political protectionism, which masks the need to deliver superior value, forgives its absence, and creates a false sense of confidence that real competition is taking place. Not only does protection discourage value, it perpetuates inferior values by enabling them to survive, suffocating the initiative to improve them while at the same time overpricing them, and inviting retaliation from producers of superior value that leads ultimately to downgraded standards of life.

The end of the industrial age and the emergence of a global economy are causing a radical reassessment of the competitive vision of many businesses and the strategies required to achieve it. Some companies are hunkered down in a survival mode while they try to figure out if there is a future for them and what that future is. They are coming up with some astonishing adjustments: A U.S. Steel with no overarching commitment to steel, an American Can without any cans, and a Singer devoid of the sewing machines that were its synonym.

The corporate soul searching that is going on is creating a new set of management precepts. We have to keep re-visioning what we are all about, managers say. What do we really do? Who benefits? How can we do it better? Should we be doing something else?

To be competitive tomorrow means that you and the other managers in your company will have to practice enormous flexibility. Either you or someone else must be constantly challenging the status quo; it is better if you do it before your competitors. Either you or someone else will be constantly coming up with new sets of standards; it is better if you do it before your competitors. Either you or someone else will be constantly trying new leadership practices, organization, and operating procedures; it is better if you do it before your competitors.

Either you or someone else will be the first to walk away from money-losing strategies or marginal businesses. Either you or someone else will achieve a new, tighter focus for a business that will give it a market leadership position. Either you or someone else will develop the new skill of running existing businesses successfully while simultaneously making significant changes in them. In all these areas, it will be better if you envision tomorrow's customers best and be the first to take the innovative steps to ensure their competitiveness.

Growth strategies such as acting as outsourcers for customer cost centers and entering into strategic alliances with them used to be the closely held province of topmost managers. In tomorrow's companies, middle-level managers are being empowered to lower their customers' costs of manufacturing and increase their percentage of high-margin sales. Their companies' growth visions tie them in tightly to customer competitiveness goals. Their leaders even speak differently about them. It used to be fashionable for leaders to say: "My job is to grow the business." The new fashion is for tomorrow's leaders to say: "My job is to grow the managers who grow our customers' businesses."

Projecting Corporate Vision Worldwide

Corporate visions, which have often been based on self-serving abstractions, will have to become founded on concrete economic calculations that specify the customer advantages that each business can deliver. Customer competitiveness, not competitor bashing, will become common to all visions as the basis of each company's mission and the source of its distribution of both funds and rewards.

Tomorrow's competitors will fight it out in a universal enterprise economy. What was once parochially called consumerist Western culture is taking over everywhere, even in such hitherto unlikely places as Eastern Europe, the Middle East, and the Soviet Union. Consumer culture is founded on the natural inclination of men and women to compete, to test themselves against others and to try to best them. It is the universalization of this culture that is making global business possible.

In a world without yesterday's trading boundaries, multinationalism has given way to globalism. Instead of a national headquarters making decisions and international business units executing them, tomorrow's competitors will not envision themselves as American, European, or Japanese. Without regard to a company's original nationality, its managers will come from anywhere, its products and services will be developed and marketed everywhere, and its political fealty may reside nowhere. Corporate sovereignty and national sovereignty need no longer necessarily be one and the same. As a result, corporate interest will not have to reflect national interest. Business policy will serve what is best for the customers of a business even when it may conflict with what is deemed to be best for its original home country.

As the nationality of companies becomes more obtuse, it will be less necessary to know where a company's managers come from or the national sources of its funds. As Peter Sprague says about his company, National Semiconductor Corporation, "We are using Russian engineers living in Israel to design chips that are made in the United States and assembled in Asia."

Daimler-Benz AG already envisions its business as a global "integrated transportation company." Its integration extends worldwide through strategic alliances of its jet aircraft engine operations with United Technologies Corporation in the United States, its helicopter business with Aerospatiale S.A. of France, and its aerospace development with Mitsubishi in Japan. Daimler-Benz intends to be internationally competitive in each area of its business. Through its alliances, it ensures a global capability in the key markets of the world. As its alliances mature and take on multibillion dollar size, it will matter less and less that Daimler-Benz is headquartered in the Black Forest outskirts of Stuttgart, Germany.

As a result of the diffusion of corporate nationality, managers are coming to see themselves as men and women of the world. In Singapore, for example, managers see their country as a natural home for international corporations. They make up their loyalties as they go along. "We can manufacture in any country in the world where there is a competitive advantage; we can make things in Thailand because the cost is low or in Germany because the market is big and we can do our R&D in Boston where scientists are in good supply. Who will care?"

Only a handful of businesses will be able to envision themselves parochially. For the rest, their situations are summed up in the words of a job-shop manager in California:

When I first came here in the 1950s, this was a nice
place to live, labor was plentiful, and I was close to my
customers. But now, my operating costs are so much
higher than competitors' halfway around the world that
I can't compete against them for customers who are
right next door to me.

In the traditional terms of product and process competition, he
has lost, defeated by competitors that he had never envisioned.

Two of the most prevalent sins of the 1980s will become high
crimes and misdemeanors in the 1990s: taking your eye off your
vision, which symbolizes the customer and his changing requirements, and protecting today's basic business at the expense of
creatively obsoleting it. Being careful instead of aggressive for
fear of tampering with success will place your business squarely
in the middle of the road where it can be passed on both sides.
As IBM among others has recognized, there will be no substitute
for becoming "the world's champion in meeting the needs of our
customers." Otherwise, no market will be safe, no manager will
be secure, and no product will endure if its contribution to
customer competitiveness lags or gets out of hand.

4

Competitive Leadership

Tomorrow's leaders will be chosen on their ability to grow their businesses by helping their customers to grow. A "good leader" will be good at making his customers more competitive. A "wise leader" will be wise in knowing who his growth customers are and how to grow them. A leader who is earning his or her pay and perks will be the leader who is helping his customers' leaders earn theirs.

The leaders who win tomorrow's competition will transcend many of yesterday's stereotypes of the rugged individual, lonely at the top, who keeps his own counsel and is ready, willing, and able to go it alone. This profile of past heroes is as dead as the dodo. In the world of lateral rather than vertical leadership and competition through cooperation and co-mangement of customer operations, a leader's paramount trait is partnerability. To be a customer peer is the first and foremost requisite for leadership.

Xerox recognized this when it was developing its Docutech system by practicing internal and external partnering right from the beginning in a way that Xerox managers acknowledge "re-shaped Xerox." Engineers, manufacturers, and marketers met monthly to play the same tune in The Symphony Group, as it became known, a format that will serve as a model for future Xerox development programs. In addition, customers were brought in early enough to serve as multiple beta sites for product use-testing.

Tomorrow's products will flow in a closed loop from the customer needs for competitive advantage that originate them to the suppliers who manufacture them and then back to the customers who will put them to work. A supplier's office and factory will be intermediaries in this process. In most cases, it will neither begin nor end with them. Before tomorrow's suppliers can do their jobs, customers will already have influenced the concepts that will become their eventual products. After they do their jobs, the application, installation, education, and consultation services that used to be considered as mere support services for products will become the main contributions to enabling products to maximize their profit contributions to their customers. The entire value chain will be reconstructed, with customer participation bookending supplier operations at both ends.

Partnerability, both inside and outside a company, has never before been a prime leadership requirement. Throughout the post-World War II years and on through the 1970s, customers were thought of as people to beat out of their money, suppliers as people to beat down on price, and competitors as people to beat. From now on, a customer's competitors will be the people to beat and customers and suppliers will be the people to partner.

In the early 1980s, it was still possible to believe that the American Century would never end. Companies could proclaim OUR CULTURE, RIGHT OR WRONG, leaders could get away with managing by wandering around their own companies instead of exploring their customers, and MY WAY OR THE HIGHWAY expressed a common management attitude toward unsolicited inputs. The belief that change was difficult provided the rationale for having as little to do with it as possible.

Proving that things weren't "broke" so that they would not have to be fixed superseded interest in change. Starting up new learning curves became a postponable purchase. While doing old things in new ways was always possible, almost every manager could say that "We ain't plowin' half as good as we know how right now." Using up that 50 percent margin gave them a long period of grace.

Throughout the 1980s, the maturing of many American industries gave birth to an infantry mentality of competitively slugging it out toe to toe, incremental change to incremental change. The equivalent of "three yards and a cloud of dust" with each try was gaining half a market share point on one or another essentially undifferentiated competitor. Competitive advantage came and went in a cyclical series of give-and-take tradeoffs until the competitors became too bored, weakened, or distracted to answer the bell for the next round. Only their customers were beneficiaries, not because they had rich, new competitive values added to them by innovation but due to the largesse of deals and discounts that were the fallouts of "marketing warfare."

It was common to see signs that read, "The guys who work the latest have the edge." Nothing was said about what they should be working on or about working the smartest along with the latest to come up with the newest, the least conformist, or the most disequalizing strategy. Putting in the "hour power," a form of serving time, often took precedence over putting in the brain power in the pantheon of values.

Reflecting Before Risk Taking

Except for the twenty years of the 1950s and 1960s, which have been called the United States' Golden Age of Invention, most corporations have to their credit pitifully few innovations that have made their customers more competitive. Most corporate growth has come from continually improving a product once it was developed, taking it step by step up the learning curve by producing progressively greater volume at lower cost. The cost savings from mass production kept paying back the added costs of upgrading. Until competitors forced innovation, driving mass producers back to the drawing boards to start all over again "with a clean sheet of paper," it was likely to be the strategy of last resort.

In industries that were national oligopolies, like steel and chemicals and automobiles, no supplier needed to innovate as long as no other supplier did. Since the end of World War II, the Big Three automakers' track record of ignored European inventions includes radial tires, disk brakes, and fuel injection while they were living off marginal improvements in their last major innovation, automatic transmission, which dates back to 1939. In just about every industry, each generation of managers tends to fall so deeply in love with the technology it creates or inherits that it sets about to perfect it rather than make the leap to transcend it for the next generation of its products.

The Boeing Company's position on innovation is "to be reflective before we take risks." Upon reflection, Boeing usually decides to update rather than innovate and to give its customers just enough of what they want to keep its airplanes salable. On the other hand, the European consortium Airbus Industrie pushes the limits of R&D. Fly-by-wire nonmechanical navigation systems, the two-pilot cockpit, fuel tanks in the tail, and composite structural materials are innovations that have all come from Airbus.

In the 1980s, new presidents could get away with keeping things pretty much the same. They could take office, look around, and—like Frank Schrontz of Boeing—decide that no major changes were needed and that life would go on. Presidents coming into capital-intensive businesses had a built-in rationale. It would be idealistic to try to change things where product lead times were five to ten years, and nothing new could come up earlier no matter what. As far as innovation was concerned, presidents who thought of themselves as simply representatives of their employees were not likely to be risk takers. Their definition of risk was narrowly constructed on the side of safety: getting involved in anything that has no history.

When market-dominating companies face up to true innovation, they frequently underachieve. General Electric's "great compressor fiasco" is an example of megacompany innovation gone awry. In spite of being a $2 billion player in the refrigerator business, GE lost track of what it calls "the magical balance between getting it right and getting it fast" when it went to market with a revolutionary compressor. A million compressors had to be replaced after repeated failures. GE took a $450 million pretax charge on its 1988 earnings as a result of what it called "your worst nightmare come true."

In the decade preceding the 1990s, a popular pasttime was to generate checklists that alleged to set down the "characteristics of excellent companies." Almost all of them agreed on the same handful of so-called excellences:

1. A bias for action, which led to the widespread formation of action teams
2. Hands-on action, which brought many leaders into participative roles
3. Lean staff, which flattened everyone's organization structure
4. Sticking to knitting, which constrained some of the more illogical extensions of innovation
5. Staying close to the customer, which opened up the early stages of customer exploration

Nowhere was partnering to be found, although some of its prehensile forerunners can be inferred from hands-on action and staying close to customers. But in tomorrow's competition, staying close will not be close enough. Only *marrying the customer* will suffice.

As long as customers are allowed to remain "out there," their closeness will always be too transient to make more than a fractional impact on your products, promotions, and prices. Tomorrow's competition will require customers to be brought into your business as resident resources just as you must become resident in your customers' businesses. *Being there* makes each of you purposefully accessible to the other without the cost-inefficiencies of amiably wandering around each other's workplaces as mutually "fractional impactionists." In a competitive environment where close is no longer good enough to partner, live-in types of exchange relationships must take place on both sides of customer-supplier and supplier-supplier relationships. Only as a live-in can you hope to claim your stake in evolving a partner's plans or stake your claim to participate in his execution of them as a contribution to your growth.

Keying on Partnering

Tomorrow's leaders will have one chance to get the vision of their customer partners straight and then to design their products and build their businesses to help their customers grow. If they envision their customer partners incorrectly, their entire business will be as wrong as the IBM PCjr computer whose manager, Don Estridge, realized as he looked back in hindsight at its failure: "We thought the machine would be used for unsophisticated uses by absolutely inexperienced first-time users." Yet 75 percent of PCjr purchasers turned out to be experienced users who were familiar with complex business software and insistent that it run on their home computers so that they could gain a competitive edge after office hours. When they found out how unsophisticated the PCjr was, the bottom dropped out of sales. "It took us by surprise," Estridge said, when it became clear not only what was happening but why.

Karl Eller made a similar mistake with his Circle K Corporation's convenience stores by not partnering with his customers when he raised prices in a customer-be-damned strategy to cover losses from operations. Circle K's mostly blue-collar customers could not stand the increase and so they stopped shopping with Eller. After Circle K's bankruptcy, its new president revealed what had taken place by admitting that "we had the attitude of gouging the customer for what we could get."

The leaders of McDonnell Douglas went on a tear in the late 1980s and booked orders for commercial aircraft at twice the pace their company could produce. Their attempt to get airplanes out the door to their airline partners made such a joke out of their employee partners' dedication to quality that the program's initials, TQMS—Total Quality Management System—became subverted to mean "Time to Quit and Move to Seattle" where archcompetitor Boeing is headquartered.

Economic Darwinists may say that such events are simply evidence of the natural selection process where resources are periodically reallocated, however involuntarily, at large companies like IBM and McDonnell Douglas and major industries like convenience store are restructured. The concept of "survival of the fittest" proves to them that if you do not make your customers more competitive, they will make you less so by taking their business to someone who will. If the waste and destruction of resources (not just their reallocation) and the human suffering this engenders is the penalty for letting nature take its course, few of tomorrow's companies will be able to afford them.

In an increasingly customer-controlled environment, where dedicated relationships will be the rule and not the exception, leaders will not have the luxury of incorrectly selecting customers to grow or incorrectly judging how to grow them. They will have to have a process for ensuring customer competitiveness. Its keystone will be partnering in close, continuing relationships of the sleeves-rolled-up kind on a full business-to-business basis in which a customer's growth and your own are correlated. Companies that offer partial partnerships, such as Hewlett-Packard's invitation to be your "technical partner," will be swept aside. So will companies whose leaders think that partnering is nothing more than the old-style arm's-length pattern of dressing up a sale here and there with the lip rouge of a pinch of free services and the eyeliner of a dash of consultation.

Joining with each major customer business manager at the hip, where joint growth plans are made, will be every leader's quintessential job. In each case, there will be three keys to become preferred as a growth partner:

1. *Customer-driven objectives.* You must learn each major customer's growth objective and make contributing to its achievement your own objective. Can you help a customer achieve his current objective on time or sooner? Can you help him outperform it? Can you make him more competitive by increasing the certainty of his achievement?
2. *Customer-supplementing strategies.* You must add the value of your own strategies to each customer's strategies so that you can supplement his competitiveness. Can you add to his value by reducing the cost of a customer strategy? Can you increase a strategy's revenue capability? Can you help ensure its success?
3. *Customer risk elimination.* You must be able to guarantee your added value so that the customer incurs no risk in partnering with you.

These three keys to partnerability add up to the requirement that you know each customer's business well enough to become a part, as in *part*ner, of it and make a significant, measurable contribution to how much the customer plans to grow it and how soon he needs to achieve results. You must put yourself on the same line with the managers of your customer businesses, their bottom line, assuming some of their responsibility in exchange for a higher proportion of their reward.

To the extent that you can take this position and deliver on it, and accumulate a track record that proves you can, you can become a leading growth partner. Your value will be measured by how much you contribute to customer competitiveness and how consistently you are able to do it.

Projecting Partnering Power

With the advent of partnering as the major leadership strategy in the new competition of tomorrow, the source of power changes. Power used to be conferred by position. In hierarchical fashion, it was applied from the top down. In some benign hierarchies, partnership was talked about but hardly ever practiced unless things got bad and all at once everybody was "all in this together" because no one wanted to be singled out as the "man who killed John."

As its middle levels have collapsed, the hierarchy has declined as the source of management power. Tomorrow's leadership skills lie in the ability to build coalitions where everybody, including the leader, is eyeball to eyeball on the same level.

Tomorrow's leaders will exercise their leadership in a world of peers and partners over whom they will have only negotiated control. They will have to be very good at networking where joint planning and joint decision making are requisite skills and internal and external competitors alike may become necessary allies. Like proverbial rug traders, leaders must always be "open to buy" divergent and dissenting points of view and make sure that the customer's voice is heard the loudest and that the customer wins. Only if the customer wins greater competitiveness can everybody else win too.

The authoritarian type of top-down power used to go by the name of policy, which was colloquially defined as "the way we do things." Tomorrow, policy will have a different definition. It will be *the way we make our customers more competitive*. Policy will no longer come from above. It will come laterally, from across, and it must be nurtured by bilateral negotiations with customer peers whose competitive advantage it is designed to accelerate.

Lateral leadership is the only kind of leadership that is conducive to partnering because it represents the only kind of power that can be put to work reciprocally by equals. Managing laterally, and projecting leadership on a horizontal rather than a vertical basis, tilts the axis of management 90 degrees, as Figure 3 shows. It provides a level playing field for you and your customers to deal, where back-and-forth negotiations can take place at eye level.

If you are positioned as an equal who practices leadership horizontally, as a customer peer, you cannot invoke your position

Figure 3. Lateral leadership.

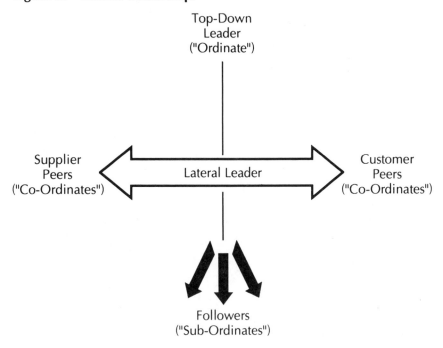

as a power generator. The only power in partnerships is proof power, the authority that comes from being able to prove how much you can improve a customer's profits, how soon you can improve them, and how sure you and your customer can be that they will be improved. You can lead customer competitiveness if you have proof power and you can have proof power only if you and your business are committed to customer growth.

In order to take leadership as the "managing partner" in your customer partnerships, you will have to work with them from an inventory of "What if?" proposals for profit improvement projects. If your "What ifs" are competitively advantageous, they will compel your customers' attention. But the only thing that will compel their buy-in will be the "then" that follows: *What if* you invest with us in improving the contribution from this business function of yours or this line of your business—*then* this is the return on your investment that you can expect; this much contribution, within this period of time and with this degree of certainty for the improvement of your competitiveness.

Leadership power in customer partnerships is going to be exclusively conferred by customers on their suppliers who are what they call "compelling": who compel them to invest where they can be most assuredly advantaged to the greatest amount in the shortest time. Compulsion is a factor of proof, because customers will not act until they are comfortable with the expectation that they will realize the results you propose and that there can be no surprises. The customer's demand to "show me" is the necessary precondition to the invitation to "partner me."

Compared to position power, which is "we-oriented," proof power is customer-focused. Instead of being able to say or act out a traditional scenario such as "*we* are the leading company and here is how *we* go about doing this sort of thing," proof power operates from a far more mutual base: "You are or want to be a leading company. We can help you maintain or grow your leadership. Here is how you are currently going about operating a critical function or business unit. Here is how we can work together with you to help improve the contribution it is making to your competitiveness. Here is how much you can expect your improvement will be. Here is how soon you can expect it to accrue. Here is its degree of certainty. Let us share our proof with you so that you can be sure enough to go ahead."

Partnering internally with your key managers will require the same sense of peerage as laterally managing your key customer and supplier relationships. Why should top-rated people work with you? You will have to give them a compelling reason that enhances their personal and professional value; in other words, just as with your customers, you will have to accelerate their competitive growth.

Why should they elect you as their sole source of employment? Can you provide them with the industry standard of incentives, support, and shared rewards so that you can claim to be their "employment supplier of choice," to be preferred above all others, and offer them an unsurpassed "quality of work life"?

Can you enable them as much as possible to *work with you* instead of *work for you?*

Can you be the leader of their charge rather than simply charge them with their own leadership?

Leading the Growth Charge

Selecting your growth partners, growing them, and being grown by them is what leading tomorrow's businesses will be all about. This three-pronged mission breaks out into managing two strategies: accelerating the growth of the major customers you are already growing and targeting prospective customers whose competitiveness you can similarly improve.

Choosing Current Customers to Partner With

There are four questions for you to answer about your current customers in order to determine which of them you can partner with for the greatest competitive advantage:

1. *Who are we growing right now?* Some of your growth partners will be customers you are already growing, yet you may not be aware of your contribution to their growth. You may think of them as core customers, key accounts, or heavy users, but they

may actually be "partners without portfolio." To determine if any one of them should be selected as a growth partner, you will have to answer three more questions:

2. *How much are they growing us?* You may be unable at the outset to know the full extent to which you are bringing growth to a current customer. But you can much more easily calculate the sum total of profits by which you yourself are growing as a result of doing business with him. There are four standards by which you should measure current customers: their absolute value as a profit maker for you, their comparative value ranked against your customer list as a whole, the rate of your profit growth, and the trend of your growth rate with them over the past three years.

3. *How much more can we grow them?* Because growth takes place in the future, sometime after you plan it, you must add a fifth standard to your calculations: What is the most likely projected rate of improved profits we can plan for in our growth of their business over the next three years? If the projected rate of growth is slowing, becoming static, or declining, you may not have a true growth partner. Instead, you may have a mature customer to whom you should sell and profit from but with whom you should not partner because no growth is possible.

4. *How much more can they grow us?* Because growth partnerships must be reciprocal, you will have to evaluate the most likely projected rate of profit growth for your own business from each customer over the next three years to see if it is increasing, becoming static, or declining. If the projected incremental rates of growth are steadily increasing for both your customer and yourself, you have a solid basis for growth partnering.

Choosing Prospective Partners

There are four questions for you to answer about prospective partners to determine which of them you should partner with for the greatest competitive advantage:

1. *Who else can we grow?* Growable customers that you are not currently growing are your source of market expansion. They

may also be a source of diversification. To qualify as a growable customer, a business must meet two criteria: It must have operating problems that are susceptible to significant cost reduction by the application of your expertise. In addition, your expertise must be able to make a significant increase in a customer's profitable sales opportunities. A prospective partner's growability can be enhanced by several factors:

o *Change at the top.* Opportunity to grow and be grown is magnified by change. A customer that is trying to become competitive or trying to become recompetitive by undergoing reorganization or restructuring is an enhanced partnership prospect. Change at the top is an added enhancement. Whenever major changes are taking place, you will have the chance to create a leadership role for yourself, meet new or newly perceived needs in new ways, and form relationships with new, upcoming customer managers whose competitiveness can benefit from your expertise.

o *Bias for partnering.* You must prefer to partner with customers who prefer to partner with you. Their receptivity to your growth proposals will be greater and so will their awareness of your impact on their costs and revenues. You should expect them to be willing to share access to their top people and operating data with you and to contribute both to making and implementing your joint growth plans.

o *Marketable Repute.* The most sophisticated customers make the best partners. They have the highest standards of performance that will drive you. They also have the most competitive leaders in their industry who will pull you and push you. They will be able to maximize your contributions to them, taking what you give them and running with it. Your odds for success will increase, as will your ability to draw on references from them that will attract other similarly sophisticated customers to you.

2. *How much will they grow us?* A business that is growable by you must also be able to grow you in return. For example, your profit volume and its projected three-year rate of growth must

meet or exceed your minimum hurdle requirements if you are to avoid opportunity loss.

3. *How can we grow them?* For each growable customer that you determine to be potentially partnerable, you must plan a growth strategy. The strategy will have to set forth the most cost-effective means by which you will add new profits to his business. You will need to specify how much profit will accrue from reducing his operating costs, how soon the flow of profits will begin, and how long they will continue to flow. You must also be able to specify the profits from new sales opportunities you will make available and the new or expanded markets they can be expected to come from.

4. *What capabilities must we invest in?* Growable customers that you are not currently growing may demand an extension of your existing capabilities. You may need to fortify your present strengths. You may also need to diversify into new strengths. Some of them may be borrowed from additional supplier partners.

Ensuring the Innovation Dividend From Partnering

Tomorrow's global market will be marked by the deadly combination of ever-costlier product development cycles and ever-shorter commercial life cycles. The costs of innovation are raised while the time over which cash can flow to recover them is foreshortened. This will be true for your customers as well as for you.

Innovation is the most precious dividend from growth partnering. The accessibility of the customer to your innovative process, partnering with his people to involve them in it, and extracting their contributions to your awareness of their needs can all act as inspirations to your development functions.

One of the basic problems of innovation in large companies may be the way research and development is done. In the United States, Kodak follows the American policy of relying heavily on technicians to perform much of the laboratory work so that scientists and engineers can spend their time thinking about the results. When the basic research is completed, the work is turned over to a development team that is responsible for translating it into new Kodak products. Except in rare cases, Kodak researchers never visit customers. In Japan, the essence of research is to put the best people in the laboratory part of the time and bring them together with customers the rest of the time so they can see firsthand what their markets need.

Tomorrow's development cycles for new products, new processes, and new materials will be stretched thin to come up with resolutions to the extremely finite and fleeting needs that highly volatile niche markets demand. This requires lengthy lead times so that you can establish a customer need yet come up with an innovative solution for it while the need's opportunity window is still open. As markets become more and more specialized, a need can be here today and different, if not gone—along with the market niche that had engendered it—tomorrow. By the time a solution is made available, the problem it solves may have disappeared.

A quick-response capability puts a squeeze on the mean time between commercializable innovations, encouraging a strategy where each innovation telescopes into the ones that precede it and follow it. No matter how revolutionary or marginal an innovation may be, the period of maximum payback will be subject to a short life by rapacious replicators in your own industry and by fickle customer standards in your markets.

More likely than not, most of tomorrow's innovations will have a fad's typical life cycle. Figure 4 shows the classic fad spike rising quickly to a peak and then, with equal velocity, falling off to the disappearing point as a major market participant. Innovations will have to have a "planned transience." The two key questions will be, How can we minimize sunk costs and how can we maximize their recovery, in both money and speed?

Every new product or service and every new business venture must be able to make a business case for its success if it only becomes a fad, even if this is its worst case. It will increasingly become a most likely case, its most probable life curve in tomorrow's markets of transiently advantaged businesses. Planning will require you to confront issues like these:

Figure 4.   Typical fad life cycle.

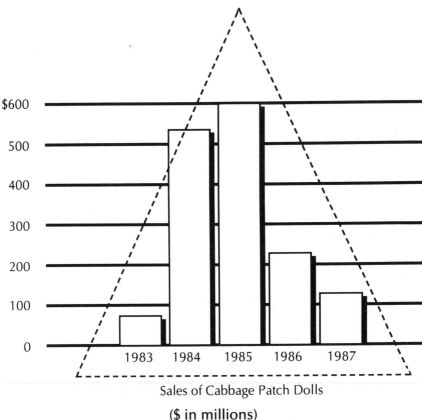

Sales of Cabbage Patch Dolls

($ in millions)

1. How small can our up-front investment be so that we can condense our payback cycle?
2. How short can our development time be so that we can condense our design cycle?
3. How fast can our market penetration be so that we can condense our commercialization cycle?
4. How quickly can we achieve full rollout at peak shipment levels so that we can condense our distribution cycle?
5. How synergistically can we coordinate our same-day shipment schedule, billing schedule, and receivables collection schedule so that we can condense our cash-flow cycle?

Innovation will be most productive for you if you take its meaning broadly, far beyond new products. If you have a customer who requires thirty-one hours to assemble a product, as General Motors did for its car assembly in 1989 when Toyota required only sixteen, you need to help him innovate his assembly lines. If you have a customer who devotes 20 percent of his plant area and 25 percent of his total work hours to reworking manufacturing defects, and his major competitor has virtually no rework areas and performs almost no rework, you need to help him innovate his production process. If your customer maintains an average of two weeks' supply of parts and his competitors get by with a supply for just two days, you need to help him innovate his inventory.

General Motors' subsidiary, Saturn Corporation, is one of the most technologically innovative companies in the world. Information technology is key to the way that Saturn cars are developed, built, distributed, sold, and serviced. Automated systems are everywhere. One system handles statistical process control, status monitoring, and maintenance management on the factory floor. Another system unites sales, service, and marketing. Saturn dealers use the system to locate cars, place orders, and check up on deliveries. Data taken from cars needing repairs go to engineers who determine if and when parts with a high repair record need redesign. In spite of all these uses of technology, GM has discovered in its joint venture with the Toyota Motor Company that it is really innovative management techniques—people working in partnership with people under a customer-concerned leadership—that contribute the single most important boost to productivity.

Innovating From Outside In

Companies that still innovate primarily from the inside out will be missing one half of the innovation equation. S. C. Johnson & Sons is an example, where Samuel Johnson has described the company's development process as "trying to listen to the marketplace . . . we have our ears open. I have set up a new products and technology department that reports to the president. It's like having a set of eyes and ears looking outside the company. . . . It's a small think tank and it comes up with thoughts by looking outside." With its staff of "marketing people, chemists, general management, and financial types," this is a vestigial development organ that goes back to the 1980s. The customer is still "outside the company," nowhere to be found inside the think tank sanctuary except through market research that may or may not be accurate, timely, or representative. In tomorrow's competition, innovation without personal customer participation will be a frivolity and a development team without regular customer members will be an anachronism.

It is not very different at 3M, where a 3Mer comes up with an idea for a new product and then forms an Action Team by recruiting full-time members from technical areas, manufacturing, marketing, sales, and "maybe finance." The Team designs the product and "figures out" how to produce and market it. From time to time, customer representatives may sit in on the Team's deliberations.

It will not be enough anymore for customers to simply sit in on your development process. They must buy in from the beginning if you are going to be able to count on them to buy in at the end. If a customer merely sits in, he will represent himself. The rest of your team will represent you. If partnership is going to have any meaning, the entire Team must represent the customer and his needs for competitive advantage. The customer must be the team's maestro rather than a back-bench auditor. Action Teams must become Advantage Teams, and the innovations they come up with must be of the customer's competitive advantage, by the customer, and for the customer.

Managers have always been better at looking inside their businesses than at looking outside them, at their markets. Innovation for customer advantage takes more than looking and listening. It requires making a customer an insider in your development department so that you can start with advantaging him his way and not just try to "figure out" how to improve his competitiveness.

The way your own development people spend their time will also be important. Bringing the customer into your development process as an insider is one step. Bringing your own people into your customers' operating processes is another. At 3M as well as many other technically driven companies, there is a 15 percent rule that allows anyone to spend up to 15 percent of each work week on anything to do with product invention. To meet tomorrow's competition, this practice will have to be updated by changing the way that alternative weeks are employed. The ideal combination would be one week with customers for every week's time on product, and there would be no way to have the one without the other. This interactive system is especially important for technical people, because it will allow them playtime in their laboratories that will be influenced by the reciprocal time they spend trying to convince customers to yield their mysteries.

For nontechnical leaders, partnering on the customer's premises can be equally beneficial. Business managers whose code of conduct has traditionally been "My job is to squeeze every bit of margin out of my business" can broaden their concept of mission by adding to it a superior commitment: "My job is to help my customers squeeze every bit of competitive advantage out of their businesses."

Staying in Front of the Newness Curve

Businesses generally develop a repute for invention when they have the greatest need for it as promising young up-and-comers in their industries. They use inventiveness as their growth platform. As they grow they lose their grasp. Whereas once they had no choice—it was innovate or evaporate—growth brings with it a difficult decision: Exploit fully what you have already developed by evolving it through successive generations of product families or dare to try to obsolete it as if you were your own competition. Once you become a leader, you tend to innovate incrementally because you have everything to lose. This exposes you to blindsiding by a breakthrough innovator who has nothing to gain by incrementing in parallel with you.

Apple Computer is often said to have defined innovativeness in the personal computer industry when it developed the Macintosh in 1984. At that time, Apple was differentiated from the computer industry leader, IBM, not only by a separate vision of the business and its customers but also by a different emphasis on ease of product use, speed, memory, expandability, and many other operating features. But in 1987, the two companies began to resemble each other. They both were envisioning the same customer, the corporate business manager. To serve him, Apple began to imitate IBM by increasing its computers' speed, power, and memory; improving their ability to integrate with IBM computers; professionalizing their hardware to meet business office standards; and offering many new software programs for office use. At the same time, IBM began to imitate Apple with enhanced graphics capability, higher resolution screens, easier-to-use hardware, and simplified instruction manuals along with new pictorial software.

Inside Apple itself, innovativeness was also undergoing change. The Mac was created by a small group of self-styled "pirates" who luckily knew "what was best" for their customers and operated as an autonomous "skunk works" that was relatively free from corporate oversight. Only five years later, the customers had moved away and the Macintosh, technically unchanged, had become obsolete. Apple had lost its vision and, as a result, its leading edge had become a trailing edge.

By 1989, several of Apple's competitors were producing computers that had more than twice the speed, half the size, and one-third the weight of the Macintosh. At that point, Apple created an innovative partnership with Japan's Sony Corporation, depending on Sony to come up with its next family of competitive products.

It is not just American managers who will have to embrace innovation partners. Managers of the German megacompanies Daimler-Benz, Bayer, and BASF have typically been as creatively inflexible as they are diligent and meticulous. In their autocratic devotion to conformity, they have often scorned internal initiatives based on independent thinking. Breakthrough innovation has never been a hallmark of the power centers of Stuttgart, Munich, and Dusseldorf or most other European companies. Products and processes, not customers, have generally been the focal points of management concern. Well-made products have been expected to sell themselves, and intelligent customers were expected to use their own initiative to figure out the best ones to buy.

Attitudes like these, which have become deeply ingrained over centuries, make many European managers reluctant to anticipate shifts in customer needs, slow to react innovatively to them, and frequently unable to take leadership of them. Instead of being pulled by their markets, they have had to be pushed, at first by the United States and then later on by Japan.

Wherever unbending systems are dictated from the top down, a damper is put on initiative. Managers under the thumb resign themselves to stay within their leaders' standards of performance and not go beyond them, keeping their desks neat, and by partnering more with their travel agents than their customers, focusing their creativity on making vacation plans.

Where patent protection has not been a factor, one to three years of high-margin grace has been about all the mileage that any company could expect to get out of an innovation in the 1970s and 1980s. This number will dwindle in the 1990s. A company that falls behind the curve of being best able to make its customers competitive can lose an entire product generation's worth of sales, together with the payback of its development costs, and it may never be able to recover in time for the next round and rejoin the race. Innovativeness is not only evidenced by product performance. It also involves reputation as the industry standard, which is even harder to reclaim than best-of-bread performance.

When Chrysler, once an innovative leader in automotive engineering, invested several million dollars' worth of national advertising to publicize independent test results that showed its cars were superior to Hondas, hardly anyone believed it. No one at General Motors changed the signs that set the standard for GM's quality control: "Honda or equal."

As less than one to three years becomes the common time frame for most industrial and technical manufacturers to capitalize on each cycle of leadership in innovation, and only several months for consumer packaged-goods makers, a new two-part scenario for consistently making customers competitive will have to be constructed: One is leadership in customer facility management or category management so that you can maintain a customer's competitiveness irrespective of whether or not you happen to have today's leading-edge product. The second part is leadership in the application and implementation of your innovativeness so that you can maximize the customer contribution of your inventions and, by getting the maximum value out of them, confront other innovators with enlarged standards to try to exceed. Their new products will have to hurdle not just your performance values but the sum of your performance plus implementation values. You may not always be able to maintain your leadership in invention. But you must never relinquish applications leadership to anyone.

No matter how hard you try, it will not be easy. On one side the predominance of a small number of megacorporations in each industry will tend to standardize products and services at parity levels and to replicate any innovative departures swiftly. On the other side, the standards themselves will be imposed by customers at their most cost-effective combinations of price and performance. These "open standards" will enforce the interchangeability of products, effectively discouraging proprietary innovations that would be incompatible with the product parallelism required for openness. Under these circumstances, many managers lack enthusiasm for experimenting with new products and processes that their customers are not clamoring for.

Customers, not suppliers, will call the innovative shots, making partnering with them inescapable. They will demand only what they need for their competitive advantage, reject excess performance and nonperforming quality, and dictate the evolution of innovation in accord with their ability to integrate it without disruption or significant retraining into their current operations.

Innovation, especially of the breakthrough kind, will become almost the sole province of microbusinesses whose existence is based on challenging megacorp standards. Yet even they will have to be careful when they threaten an accelerated obsolescence of customer asset bases. Disorder and disintegration of up-and-running operating systems may be too high a price to pay for a customer to be the first kid on the block with something new.

Leading the Nonnational Geobusiness

As a result of transnational mergers, joint ventures and alliances, acquisitions, and global outsourcing by every country's domestic suppliers, companies all over the world are progressively losing their national identities. They will actually be more than simply international and doing business everywhere; they will be nonnational and owing their allegiance nowhere. Headquarters will become an arbitrary floating point, unfettered by logistics or psychological considerations so that it can be set up just about anywhere real-time communications in voice, data, and images are available. The lateral scope of leadership partnering will be as broad-banded as the earth itself.

The airline and automobile industries have already gone nonnational. Even before the 1980s had ended, British Airways (BA) had bought a 15 percent stake in United Airlines, making United no longer exclusively an American corporation. Although still based in the American heartland of the Midwest, United's domestic vision has become partnered with BA's world mission; in turn, BA is becoming Americanized by its relationship with United. As the combined airline's operations become increasingly widespread, its leadership can come from anywhere.

Air France and Lufthansa have also taken preliminary steps to become nonnationally organized. They share a joint computer system to handle air freight shipments and they cooperate in training pilots, scheduling routes, and maintaining catering services. Their managers rotate between the two companies. Yet they remain independent businesses, retaining their corporate identities and competing against each other. Iberia and American Airlines are additional cooperative marketing members of the Air France-Lufthansa alliance.

Partnering across multiple national cultures is replacing partnering among corporate cultures as the neatest trick of the week for tomorrow's leaders. Yet there will be no way to lead a truly global business without this kind of multilateralism. It takes various forms in each industry. In the automobile business, Honda's leaders have set up a worldwide company that sells more cars in the United States than its original parent company sells in Japan. In addition, Honda America exports cars for sale back to Japan, as well as to other countries. As the power balance within Honda shifts to the American company, which was originally set up as a traditional subsidiary, the historical fact of Honda's Japanese ancestry will become less meaningful.

Honda, liked United and American Airlines, has no reason to care where in the world its sales are made any more than it cares where its profits come from or where they go in the form of investments to make new profits. Honda managers react to opportunity, which recognizes no boundaries except those of their vision.

Unlike the multinational companies of the 1980s, leaders of nonnational geobusinesses position themselves as professional managers, partnering ubiquitously and urging their partners to forget where their companies and their partners' companies once originated. All of them are equal opportunity partners who are equally opportunistic.

When Citicorp or Sumitomo or Deutschebank takes leadership in financing a global investment, neither the money nor its managers may be American or Japanese or German. When customers buy a Honda, the car may be either American or Japanese. When passengers fly United Airlines, it will be neither an American nor a British airline. With customer-standardized quality of performance, business will go to the leader who is best able to reach out and partner.

5

Competing Vertically

Tomorrow's competition will be vertical competition, a struggle for market niches and for niches within niches. Segmentation and subsegmentation will be the essence of marketing. The marketer who subsegments best—who can core and recore a market to target the heaviest needers of each specific type of competitive advantage who will pay a premium price for it—will be the most advantaged competitor himself.

As mass markets atomize, fragment, and splinter into segments, the business policy of every supplier will have to change from horizontal scanning to intense vertical focus. No longer will it be commercially feasible to try to get small shares of business from large numbers of customers. The only way to make money in the 1990s will be to concentrate on getting an ever-growing share of each of a relatively small number of customers. This fact of life will make vertical marketing the hands-down strategy of choice.

The meaning of verticalization is that middle-of-the-road products and services, the market spanners that try to straddle multiple market segments, will be increasingly at risk. Each of them will make an implicit invitation to be niched. Tomorrow's most dangerous phrases will be those that include references to "*the* market." Managers will be able to speak only of and for specific market segments. Each market segment will assemble for a time around a particular mix of benefits, then reassemble around another mix that may be only marginally different, in a ceaseless flow of varying speeds, irregular timing, and ungovernable directions. "Owning a market" will mean it reenfranchises you almost daily, coming forward and declaring once again the compelling nature of your added values.

Tomorrow's competition will be the beginning of the end of many multiline, multiproduct, and multimarket businesses that have been trying to be "all things to all people." Only businesses that are everything or something special to some people will be moneymakers. For the rest their moneymaking businesses will no longer be able to subsidize the others that cannot pull their own weight. No industry, whether manufacturing or service, will escape. They will all echo the statement made by Aetna Life & Casualty Company when it exited several types of insurance businesses: "There was a time when this company wanted to write every type of policy in all fifty states. We just don't want to do that any longer."

Along with other companies that have taken pride in all the market segments they are in, Aetna is putting each of its businesses to a litmus test: a return of 15 percent or it goes out.

Verticality, going straight down to the core of a cohesive market, will be tomorrow's only marketing direction that can expect to hit paydirt. No supplier will be able to sustain competitive superiority in any horizontal benefit.

Tomorrow's competitors will be involved in a perpetual market-narrowing process. Broad, deep mass markets have become relics of the past. The Pareto principle will dominate market segmentation, reminding you that fewer than 20 percent of all your customers in any market can account for more than 80 percent of your profits. These are your core customers, the heavy needers and therefore the heavy profit contributors. They may or may not be the same as your high-volume customers, but they constitute your core market as far as your profits from sales are concerned.

The remaining 80 percent or so of all your customers may

yield as little as 20 percent or less of all your profits. They are the source of a disproportionate amount of your costs, excessively expensive to identify, to convert, and to serve.

Mass markets have always been a hodgepodge. They contain heavy users and light users mixed in with heavy and light profit contributors. Many of the heaviest users are light profit contributors because they buy on price. In contrast, light users who buy on value can be heavy profit contributors. All mass markets contain customers who could be divested without loss. Customers who cost more to serve than they contribute could be divested at a gain.

Hodgepodge markets have become an unaffordable liability. They, along with the volume-based businesses that supply them, are being downsized for restructuring in market after market. Without downsizing, the costs of marketing volume—inventorying it, warehousing it, distributing it, selling it, collecting on it—would overwhelm profits. Instead of yesterday's mission of providing "something for everybody," the basic marketing guideline for tomorrow must be "something for somebody" or "everything for somebody." Growth in the 1990s will be the result of progressive market narrowings to find your core "somebodies."

Preparing to Niche or Be Niched

Being tomorrow's market leader implies more and more the responsibility to niche or be niched. If you try to defend a mass market everywhere, you will be strong nowhere. You will lose where your competitors choose to be strong. They will be strong where they have chosen to be the specialists.

Nichers are able to segment out their niches from mass markets because they position themselves as the new standard-bearers, holders of the most cost-effective norms for achieving a competitive advantage. Niching is a response to the nichers' challenge: Compare our norms with your current performance, nichers say to their customers; wherever our ability to reduce one of your costs is more advantageous to you than your current capability, or our ability to increase your revenues and earnings is advantageous, ask us how you can acquire our added values.

When a market mobilizes around a set of superior values that are specific to its needs for competitive advantage, it is niched.

In tomorrow's competition, you will have no alternative but to niche others before they niche you. An accurate vision of what constitutes a marketable niche must be your guide in segmenting your competitors' markets and knowing when to suspect that your own markets may be segmented against you. Two criteria will help you:

1. Do customers in the segment have the kind of profit improvement opportunity that you are capable of growing best?
2. Are these customers capable of growing you best in return?

The first question tells you if you can be a market's specialist. The second question tells you if the market can be a growth opportunity for you. The answers to both questions depend on the margins each of you can generate for the other.

Market narrowing begins with the customers who are your current "20 percenters" of profit contribution. They form the base of your near-term future business. They assure you a high rate of unit profits on sales because they have already discovered their ability to benefit competitively from doing business with you. In many cases, they have quantified your added value, compared it with your price, and classified you as a bargain—as a source of value that is greater than its cost.

Price has lost its discriminatory role for them. Your margins have come to represent a fair trade-off for competitive advantage.

A 20 percent type of customer who pays premium margins is telling you something: You are growing him. The values you are adding to his profits, either by reducing his operating costs or increasing his profitable sales revenues, are accelerating his growth. He is willing to pay you for the value of the new profits you are supplying.

The first commandment for tomorrow's competitors is to grow your business with the customers whose growth you are already improving. The second commandment is to search out and serve prospective "twenty percenters" you are not currently growing but whose businesses you are equally able to grow. Taken together, these two customer groups will form your *growth niche*.

Niching is the order of the day in every major market. In retailing, one of the oldest industries, merchants are de-departmentalizing stores into "focus boutiques," restructuring their multiproduct outlets into specialty "stores-within-the-store" or freestanding self-contained specialty centers that serve specific niche customers.

Carson Pirie Scott operates three stores-within-the-store. One specializes in the youth niche, another in the homemaker niche, and a third in the business executive niche. Montgomery Ward has converted its general merchandise stores into self-contained specialty stores that serve the home and automotive markets. Sears has organized a separate chain of Business Systems Centers that sell computers. KMart operates specialty home centers and a separate chain of drug retailers. Warehouse-type specialty stores are all over the country, catering to the home improvement market niche or majoring in home electronics.

Specialty stores are exclusively driven by their markets. They can flexibly respond to changes in customer tastes for styles or fashions and even anticipate them at times. Their return on equity shows the result. It averages almost 30 percent, double the 15 percent that is the traditional average for top department store companies.

Niching is a strategy without end. Even within already-niched categories, progressive verticalization generally continues. "Category killers," specialty discounters who focus on a single product category like toys, electronics, or books, are niching the discount department stores. Killers like Toys "Я" Us offer wider selections at greater price cuts than the Wal-Marts, KMarts, and Targets they have cored. In response, the Big Three of discounting have begun to purchase category specialists such as sporting goods stores.

Retailers' catalogs are also becoming niched. Sears has two dozen "specialogues," each of which focuses on a specific market like power tools, toys, and petite clothing. Spiegel publishes more than thirty different catalogs. Montgomery Ward, on the other hand, has gone out of the catalog business after 113 years. It refused to niche its general catalogue.

Segmenting on a Two-Tier Platform

Tomorrow's competitive leadership begins with the market-narrowing question, *Who can we grow?* There are two answers: customers who right now are paying unnecessary direct costs to run operations in their major business functions where you are process smart or customers who are paying the unnecessary opportunity costs of unrealized sales in their major markets where you are sales smart. To be competitive tomorrow demands that the monolithic concept of a universal market, thought of as being composed of equally valuable customers, be divided into a two-tier segmentation.

The first segment, the top tier, is composed of your growing and growable customers. You are a major source of their competitiveness. The second tier is composed of "all others," the 80 percenters who contribute the remaining 20 percent of your profits. The top tier will grow you. The bottom tier challenges your ability to sell to it in the most cost-effective manner. How low can you make your cost of sales? How effectively can you manage each customer relationship at that cost so that you can maximize your earnings at minimal expense?

Your top-tier business is your "branded" business. It will make you competitive. Your bottom-tier business is a commodity business. It will supplement your earnings. It will not be your growth source nor will you be a major growth source for its customers.

Your market tomorrow will resemble the pyramid shown in Figure 5. The top tier is your growth country. While small in size, it possesses a disproportionate power to grow you. The bulk of the pyramid is your slow-growth and no-growth country. Large in size but powerless to drive growth, it will ensure perpetual noncompetitive status for you if it remains the focus of your business strategy.

In managing a two-tier market, you will have to avoid the line of least resistance, which is to go on doing what you have

Figure 5. Two-tier market pyramid.

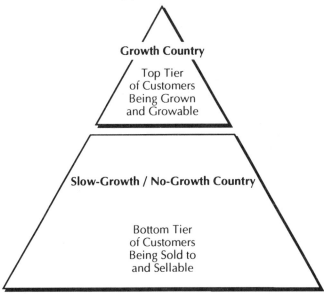

been doing but to do it a little bit better. This would concentrate your business attention on increasing volume to become a market share leader among your 80 percenters. This strategy will guarantee slow growth by diffusing your proper focus on growing your most profitable customers, the 20 percenters.

The top-tier market, composed of the customers you can grow best, is the market niche where you excel. It is the arena of your greatest expertise: your version of "Our Game." If you cannot grow your customers and yourself by playing your game—doing what you can do best—you cannot grow at all. The art of maximizing competitiveness is always to lead with your premier growth skills.

The customer segments you can grow are predetermined by what you are good at. What you are good at, in turn, should be predetermined by the needs of the customers you can grow.

If you are a data processing systems supplier, your game centers on improving customer profits by applying information technology to their most critical business functions. When you apply your technology to their inventory control and warehousing functions, you can reduce their costs. When you apply your technology to their credit and collection functions, you can increase their revenues. These become the strategies by which you grow your customers. Your most growable customers will be the businesses that depend most heavily for their success on the functions you can improve. Several data processing suppliers have already found their games and, along with them, their niches:

Company	Niche
NCR	Retailing
Control Data	Science and engineering
Honeywell	Process control
Burroughs	Retailing and finance
Sperry	Government
Qantel	Professional football and basketball

Picking, Choosing, and Servicing Your Niches

Few niches are ever so specific that they cannot be further niched. In order to compete against NCR in its retail market niche, IBM has identified more than forty market segments such as accounting, automobile repair shops, and beauty salons. IBM wants each of its personal computer dealers to focus on a few of them, catering to their specific needs with specialized systems of hardware, software, and services. At Apple Computer, dealer specialization is also a critical element of long-term strategy.

In order to play your game, you may have to move away from your traditional customer base if you cannot grow it enough to maximize the profits that you need to grow you in return. You will have to seek out new growth markets. These may consist of different industries or smaller, more entrepreneurial businesses than you are accustomed to serve, whose demands can be different, both in the frenzy of their pace and in their nature. They may even be businesses in a different market that have different cost structures and different customers than you are used to. Yet if you want to be one of tomorrow's competitors, you may be forced to re-niche your top-tier market. The alternative can be stark: You and your historical markets may decline, decay, and divest in concert.

There is an acid test for successful niching: You are your market's standard of value. The value you standardize cannot be a product or service. It must be customer growth in the form of new profit dollars. This is the only value for which customers will consistently pay you a premium price. In turn, the premium price they pay will be the basis of your own growth.

This is what "positioning" is all about. Either you are positioned as being the standard of your market's value or you are not positioned for maximum growth. There is no other way to grow. Since no-growth or slow-growth is a recumbency and not an active posture, there is no other positioning.

Cooper Tire & Rubber Company knows how to be a niche player in the automobile aftermarket. Cooper focuses on the replacement tire business, avoiding competition with Goodyear, Bridgestone, and Michelin, who fight among themselves for the right to sell original equipment tires at discounted prices to automotive manufacturers. Over the 1980s, Cooper increased profits at a compound rate of 22 percent annually by specializing in serving independent tire dealers that account for nearly two-thirds of all replacement sales in the United States. Cooper has become the industry standard for the independents because it focuses its business on them, does not have its own competitive retail outlets, and will privately label its tires with each independent's own name.

In the early 1990s, International Paper Company had $9 billion in revenues and an average return on equity of 6.5 percent. One-twentieth its size, the P. H. Glatfelter Company had a comparable return of 20.3 percent because, it says, "We've picked and chosen the markets we can service best and we service the hell out of them." In the brokerage business, A. G. Edwards, Inc., at $500 million had a return on equity of 17 percent against the $12 billion Merrill Lynch's 11 percent, with profit margins four times greater than those of Merrill. Edwards spends its time "figuring out how to provide better services to existing retail customers instead of looking for new areas of financial services to enter."

Marketing on the Margins

Tomorrow's competitive edges will be thinner and briefer, harder to come by, and harder to hold onto. As a result, each advantage will be marginal and will prevail for only a marginal amount of time. That is one definition of the new marginality, emphasizing the slim and fleeting nature of competitiveness. There is a second definition that focuses on margins as the manipulator of profits. This foretells that margin advantages will be found almost exclusively in niche markets, where earnings per unit of sale are more important than volume in determining profits.

Competition Based on the Margins of Advantage

Competition based on the margins of advantage brings a new focus to business. From the 1960s to the 1980s, it was difficult enough to answer the customer question "What have you *done* for me lately?" In the 1990s, the question is different and an answer even more difficult to come by: "What have you done for *me* lately?" which reflects the need for each customer segment's— and each customer's—individual advantage.

Customers endlessly look for an edge, however precarious or temporary. A small edge in cost control for a business function here, a small edge in margin control for a line of business there, will be tomorrow's leading compelling "products." Some supplier will be the best at providing each type of edge; he will be able to deliver it fastest or in the greatest amount or most reliably. As his reward, he will own the market segment for whom the edge is a critical factor in its success. When the edge no longer affords its customers a competitive advantage, either because it has been equaled or surpassed or another edge has become more urgently needed, the supplier may lose his own edge to another segmenter. He will have been niched.

Niching markets for transient marginal edges is tomorrow's basic marketing strategy. Niches will always be in the process of becoming more sharply defined. When a niche shrinks, the competitive edge it requires will become more marginal and the ability to base its competitiveness for any length of time on each edge will be more tentative. Just as the universal concept of "the market" has become irrelevant, its companion concept of "sustainable competitive advantage" is equally obsolete. If an advantage is competitive, it cannot be sustainable; if sustainable, it will be a commodity that cannot determine competitiveness.

The act of creating transient, marginal edges for your markets is the true test of your ability to be a craftsman in either a product's original design or its custom fitting to your customers' operations through your applications expertise. On the customer's side, the art of putting a transient, marginal edge to work before it becomes mature—which means that its exclusivity has come and gone—or before it loses its edge—which means that its advantage has been superseded—will be the key to competitiveness. Speed is the essence on both sides of every supplier-customer partnership.

Marginal competition is a battle for temporary supremacy in your ability to supply successive incremental improvements in customer profits. The sum of a customer's total increments adds up to his growth. You should look for breakthroughs into exponential growth as always possible but unpredictable. But the S-curves engendered by breakthroughs will themselves be increasingly transient, culminating in foreshortened life cycles that can begin to condense far sooner after payback—or even before it—than you may have planned.

Competing for Advantageous Margins

Because niche markets are smaller than mass markets, they cannot promise mass-based volume as their source of earnings. But because they require successive incremental edges that they are able to convert into competitive advantages, they are ready, willing, and able to pay premium prices to obtain them. As a niche marketer, you will have tomorrow's only opportunity to maximize your margins short of breakthroughs.

Margins, not revenues, are where niche profits must be made. Competitive market niching must be driven by *margin mania*, a zeal for maximum unit earning power. Without the crutch of volume, there is no way to "make up for" discounted prices or "freebie" deals that attempt to disguise them.

Managing Exploding Prices, Products, and Channels

Niche prices originate with a niche's customers. This means that
there is no price that can be put on a nicher's product until its
value to each of his customer's businesses has first been calculated. Each value is customer-specific. Consummate nichers, as a
result, do not publish price lists. Nor do they sell products off the
shelf from catalogs. They ask customers for an investment, not a
price, that is commensurate with the value they receive.

On the shelf, your products represent only costs. By installing them, applying them, and consulting on their application,
you can turn their costs into values. Partly through the performance of your products but mostly through the customer knowledge and applications expertise of your people, you can come
into a market you have niched and create individualized values
that have not been there before. When you have finished, your
customers will have achieved greater competitiveness.

In tomorrow's competition, technological flexibility and the
increasing diversity of distribution channels will make it possible
for every niche, no matter how small (in many markets, this will
mean right down to the number of one) to have its own customized product or service. The marketing issue for suppliers is how
to make it pay. This requires immense production flexibility,
allowing small custom runs to be made economically by means of
rapid, affordable changeovers plus highly market-specific, direct
channeling of distribution and targeted promotion.

Continuing channel explosion will mark tomorrow's competition. The number and types of segmented gateways to niche
markets will proliferate and personalize along with their products
as they become increasingly segment-driven and segment-spe-
cific. Customer access to products and services will emphasize
convenience and immediacy, making distribution necessary not
only on a just-in-time basis but also on the basis of products and
services flowing to their customers rather than the other way
around. The "when" of distribution will be when a customer
wants it. The "where" will be as much as possible where customers will want to use it.

In the 1980s, point of warehousing, point of manufacture,

point of sale, and point of use were just beginning to come closer together. Tomorrow's points of sale and use will often merge. Orders and reorders will be largely automated, converting the roles of salespeople to specialized services like custom application, installation, implementation, education, and consultation rather than taking orders or ensuring that goods and services are available. Sellers will have to do more than "know their customers" and how to reach them; they will have to live *with* their customers and live *as* their customers to envision their new demands in real time as these demands occur and take them on the rise.

Many personal sales forces of the 1980s proved to be highly cost-ineffective distributors for low-margin, undifferentiated commodity products and services. They added unretrievable costs to sales and frequently could not pay their way. Tomorrow, commodity sales forces will be unaffordable. Commodity lines will have to use unpeopled channels for their distribution, such as automatic order and reorder systems, or telemarketing and direct-by-mail sales and distribution, which allow a small labor force to serve a large number of customers at a low cost of sale. Meanwhile, peopled sales forces will be selling to their top-tier niches. Many of tomorrow's top-tier salespeople will be in permanent residence with their customers where they can add their values in the form of on-line advice, information, and counsel on applying the products and services they represent to a customer's operations. In this role, people will be irreplaceable no matter how well they may be supplemented by computerized databases, artificial intelligence programs, or telecommunications access to remote sources of knowledge.

Personalized, individualized distribution is a natural accompaniment of the personalized products that result from niche customization. A working model of tomorrow's distribution is the telefaxed newspaper that comes directly into each subscriber's home or office. It is composed only of the sections that a subscriber has specifically requested to meet his or her interests and is progressively updated twenty-four hours a day instead of only in the historic form of "editions." Undelivered by human hands, the "faxpaper" is paid for on a monthly bill as if it were another utility like light and heat rather than a considered or impulse purchase. *"The* newspaper," like *the* market, will be superseded by *"my* newspaper."

The concept of *the customer as market* will continue to be pioneered by media, many of which are from inception already market-niched. *Financial Weekly* magazine is experimenting with a toll-free telephone service that can hook up a reader with his closest car dealer or computer store if he wants to follow up on advertisements that have moved him. Time Warner advertisers in its *Time, People, Money,* and *Sports Illustrated* magazines can run personalized ads that address individual subscribers by name and supply the names and addresses of dealers who are located near their homes or workplaces. In Time Warner's vision, "The future of communications is narrowcasting."

In the fast-food business, "quick and convenient" is no longer competitively compelling. Tomorrow's customers are demanding extensive product variety and customization to accommodate a broad spectrum of personal tastes. In addition to stand-up eating, they also want sit-down restaurants, mobile units that bring the food to them, and toll-free hot lines to order in. Fast-food merchants are also being required to explore enhanced uses of technology to automate their cooking and service operations in order to reduce the range and frequency of variations from their advertised standards.

The principal value of people in the distribution channels of tomorrow's competition will be to create as much of this type of intense personalization as possible for all products and services and to counsel with customers to help them extract every ounce of value for their competitive advantage.

Sounding Taps for Loyalty

Vertical competition is the individual consumer's "nirvana." He or she becomes significantly enhanced whenever competitive suppliers make each customer their highest common denominator of product and service satisfaction. At once, individual needs, wants, and desires can be catered to in an increasing number of cases on a one-to-one basis, almost as if each customer is the sole customer. The net result of acute verticalization is that the end user becomes the product developer for competitive sources of supply. His or her work style and life-style are the R&D laboratories in which needs are annealed into product prototypes and released to manufacturing.

Customers are not only able to act as their suppliers' product developers and designers. By accessorizing products according to their individual fancies, customers are also serving as their suppliers' subassemblers. Low-end cars are often ordered fully packed with accessories, "loaded" in automotive terminology. They can cost more than high-end luxury cars and can be a good deal more luxurious. Their extra initial cost and ongoing costs of ownership have been cancelled out, however, by a third fact of economic life: the added value of individualization.

The niche markets of tomorrow's competitors will be loyal to one thing and one thing alone: to the most specialized added value they can get their hands on—specialized in the sense of being specially advantageous to their competitiveness. In the same way that nichers restlessly seek out market holes to fill, the customers who are penetrable through these holes are persistently searching out new values. In their search, they are not supplier-specific or product-specific but value-specific. When they find a competitively advantageous value, they quantify it to their satisfaction and then qualify its supplier as a reliable source. When these two criteria are met, they buy.

In doing so, they are being loyal to their mission of becoming and remaining the most advantaged competitors in their industry. If they move away from your share of their market, you may be inclined to say that they are being disloyal to you. They, however, will feel that you have not kept faith by continuing to update your customized value to them. They will perceive that it is you who have been disloyal, not them. You will be seen as having allowed yourself to become competitively disadvantaged, forcing them to accept the same fate. Loyalty, they will tell you, works both ways.

Loyalty to the best competitive advantage, the highest, timeliest, and surest value, is the only basis on which you can grow tomorrow's business. Either you supply reliable compelling values or you will be pre-empted, left holding the bag containing a hollow cored-out market.

Paradoxically, the most "disloyal customers"—those who are loyal to the best competitive advantage no matter who supplies it—are the customer niches that you should covet the most. As a result of being the most competitively advantaged in their own markets, attracting and serving the highest-margin customers of their own, they will form your most profitable demand base.

"High-potential disloyals" is the most accurate classification you can give your most important sources of growth funds. It will remind you of their propensity to be *value migrants*, in perpetual motion toward or away from you based on their satisfaction with the current incremental value you represent to their competitive advantage. It will also remind you of your vulnerability to being niched if you let your value down.

Within and among niches, volatility is marketing law. This will make tomorrow's markets extremely dynamic and foster progressive innovation as the sine qua non of your business growth. In the 1980s, managers liked to say that 30 percent of their product portfolio at any given time did not exist three to five years earlier and that 60 percent of their profits were derived from new products.

It is just as likely that the same kind of comments may be applicable to tomorrow's market portfolios.

6

Competing on Value

Tomorrow's competitors must count on being qualitative equals. Year by year, each competitor will come closer to achieving product parity at similar high standards of performance that will approach six sigma, virtual perfection at the 99.9997 level with a defect rate of only 3.4 per million. As a result, with parity in product quality and almost total quality control as a universal standard, product quality will progressively disappear as a competitive advantage. It will no longer differentiate suppliers in any compelling way. A quality standard of 99.9998 will be no more competitively advantageous to your customers, and will therefore not act as a discriminant for them in selecting you as a partner over 99.9996. Neither will it be worth paying more for.

As the quality of original equipment has improved under the mass "Total Quality" campaigns of the 1980s, everybody's Maytag Man faces technological unemployment, and the replacement parts business in many industries is dying. Only extraordinary circumstances will alter this generalization. Until the record-breaking nationwide heat waves of the summer of 1990, for example, the replacement automobile radiator business was well on its way to becoming a memory.

In many cases, product quality at near-perfect levels will exceed customer requirements for "good enoughness," which represents the optimal level of value that a customer needs to achieve, maintain, or regain competitive advantage. Good enoughness represents a customer's "point of sufficient return." It is shown on Figure 6 as the point where you have made 80 percent or so of your progress toward satisfying customer requirements for value. If you try to achieve theoretical perfection by going the remaining 20 percent of the way, it can cost you up to 80 percent of your total investment. Even if you get there, your customers may remain unimpressed. Your quality, now maximized instead of optimized, may exceed their needs. Your price may exceed their ability to make the excess quality pay or pay back. You may be left in the unenviable position of being the high-cost supplier. If a customer pays your price, he may put himself in the same position with his own markets.

Figure 6.   Good-enoughness curve.

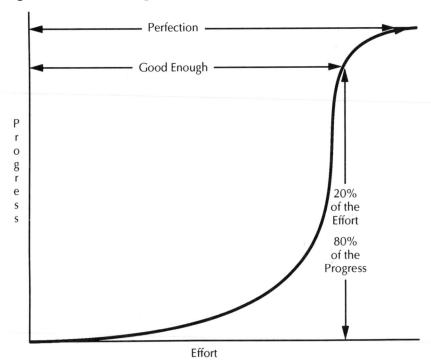

The 1980s made clear that you could not manufacture your way into competitive preference. Without enough quality, you could not compete. But with enough quality, you could not win simply by having more-than-enoughness.

The search for excellence is nothing but trouble. Even when it can be attained, best is often the enemy of good enough. Searching for the best after good enough has been achieved only dissipates scarce human cognitive resources and runs out the clock on being first to get through an opportunity window.

Motorola's "obsession with quality" (which it defines as technological excellence at the six sigma level) has gone so far beyond good-enoughness that it has been blamed for squandering the company's lead in marketing new microchip products. Alongside the Malcolm Baldrige National Quality Award, Motorola's competitors have awarded it the booby prize for demanding that its engineers create the best-designed, fastest, and highest quality chips before it will ship a single one of them. In the meantime, its competitors have been stealing the show by taking away Motorola's customers. Unisys gave up waiting and did its business with Intel Corporation. Hewlett-Packard waited so long that it missed the market window for one of its major computer workstation lines. Eventually HP had to use its own chips.

In tomorrow's competition, good-enoughness is being legislated by customer standards of product performance to which all suppliers must conform. The standards are uniformly high and highly uniform. Deviations one way or the other, either up or down, receive short shrift because they cannot pass through a customer's decision-making process. Open standards will eventually prevail everywhere so that every product's seamless fit into integrated systems with other products and into already-installed customer operations will be mandatory.

As customer-imposed "open systems" become standard throughout industry, each supplier will be confronted with the problem of how to differentiate his products in an environment where things equal to customer standards will be equal to each other. Under enforced commoditization, some companies are looking backwards for a solution. In this instance, IBM represents a typical point of view with its opinion that "We can do that by the breadth of our offerings and application of superior technology with a clear view of our customer requirements." Product line breadth will merely compound the problem. Only superior applications *values*—not superior technology—will have a chance of breaking through standardization and calling attention to a meaningful difference in the ability to deliver nonstandard customer satisfaction.

In IBM's industry, all the major players are convinced that survival will be based on owning their own technology even though its performance is standardized by customer fiat. They see technology ownership as the only way to control their destiny. Yet technology will only give them a tool kit. The experience and expertise in applying it to make their customers more competitive will be the true resource worth owning. Everything else will be buyable and partnerable. Tomorrow's destiny lies in applications since it is only through application of a technology's features that their benefit values will be able to be installed in customer operations. Installing value requires labor intensity at high levels of customer knowledge as well as technical proficiency. Whoever controls the best applications labor force will control the customer.

Once it became apparent that product performance was going to have to be equalized at high levels according to customer mandate, quality began to recede as a discriminator of purchase.

Competitiveness was going to have to be based on other factors whose point of departure is the assumption that all competitive products are almost always going to be good enough. Accordingly, superiority can no longer be won in manufacturing. Nor can preeminence be held for long by it, because the cycle time of replication has shortened everywhere. Breakthroughs as a way around the standardization of quality have become increasingly expensive, technologically problematic, and full of negative implications for the economics of a customer's management of the bought-and-paid-for assets of his installed base.

Some of the companies that have already perceived the ways in which winning tomorrow will be different from having won yesterday are acknowledging that the basis for customer satisfaction is shifting to non-product-related factors, along with the entire thrust of competitiveness. They are changing their mindsets but are in midpassage in altering their vocabulary. Quality, once reserved to mean strict conformity to product standards, has become increasingly elasticized to cover everything that you and your people do to make "a measureable impact on the satisfaction of customer needs." Quality has expanded into "Total Quality," but even in its enhanced form it is still largely product oriented. The truth comes out in the thinking of people like those on the Malcolm Baldrige National Quality Award committee who place customer satisfaction seventh and last on the Baldrige checklist of what they mean by quality.

Using Equal Quality as the Starting Point

When customer-specified equality defines quality, defect-free products will be run of the mill. They will be expected, relegated to being one of the basic requirements for competing rather than a competitive advantage. Competitive product inequality will keep you from getting a foot in the door. But once in, quality will act merely as your entry fee. All it will do is to allow you to line up for the race. At that moment, the real competition begins. The winner will be the supplier who delivers the highest *quantity* of customer value.

Quality is what goes into your products and how you sell and support them. Value is what your customers get out of everything you do. Manufacturing-based companies cherish the belief that they build in value. They do not. They build in cost.

To compensate for it requires more than zero defects. It requires a dedication to help customers maximize their ability to extract value by training them and supplying them with education along with applications expertise, operating information, project management, and consultation. These are the capabilities that will make tomorrow's competitors valuable.

A company that achieves six sigma in its manufactured quality can still suffer competitive disadvantage unless it can also help its customers achieve six sigma in their value-extracting capabilities. On the other hand, a company with six sigma standards as an applier and counselor will be competitively advantaged over any other company that lacks them no matter how qualified its products may be.

Tomorrow, only customer value will be marketable. This will not be the warm and fuzzy "perceived value" of the 1980s but demonstrable, provable, hard-numbered value. Instead of Zenith saying, "The quality goes in before the name goes on," companies may prefer to claim, "The value comes out when the product goes in a customer's application."

The true measure of value is customer satisfaction, which is based on applied value. Satisfaction takes place in customer operations, not yours. It reflects a customer's competitive advantage, not an advantage that you may claim for yourself because you have raised one more integer on the right of the decimal point in measuring your quality. Satisfaction measures your customer's added value—how much more competitive he is, and how much less of a high-cost producer or how much more of a high-margin supplier, as a result of doing business with you.

Products will be a drag on the market, especially those that are undifferentiated at equally high levels of quality. Very few companies will want to be stuck making mostly commodity products. Many of them are already saying something like "Our objective is to steadily reduce the percentage of our total sales represented by products that are purely commodities." Unfortunately, they are going about it in a way that owes more to history than to tomorrow, trying to come up with products that are unique enough to be differentiated but still not so unique that they fall outside the open standards for interconnectability that are imposed by customers. Even when companies succeed, few of them will be able to hold onto their uniquenesses very long or sustain differentiation for enough time to derive substantial profits. In their focus on product innovation, not enough companies are exploring unique applications whose values can provide a significant cost or revenue advantage to their customers. Yet tomorrow's high margins will be far more likely to come from applications expertise than from product exclusivity.

In the words of William Anders, chairman of General Dynamics Corporation, "Engineering *über alles* is a thing of the past."

Knowing Where to Add Your Value

If you go too far into tomorrow's competition without knowing the values you contribute to your customers, you will be committing yourself to being noncompetitive. You may become unrescuable. You must know the current values of the customer business functions and lines of business to which you want to add value. You must know how much value you can add to your customers and how soon they are most likely to achieve it. You must let them know how certain they can be—not how certain *you* are— that the value you propose will be the actual value that will accrue to them. This means that you must become expert in adding value and in knowing how you add value, when you add it, and how much you add. You will also have to know where to add your value, concentrating it in the two areas of each customer's business that determine his competitiveness:

1. Enhancing the margin or turnover rate of one of a customer's most crucial *revenue generators*
2. Reducing the expense of one of a customer's most crucial *cost contributors* that affect the most crucial revenue generators

These guidelines say to put your money where your customer's money is, in the operations where most of his competitive advantage currently comes from and the applications on which it is most dependent.

Competing on value requires you to compute your proposed impacts on the revenue generators or cost contributors that you affect. How much profit will you add? How soon will it begin to flow? How long before it fully accumulates? How sure is it? These questions all ask for quantification, not narrative estimates.

Within this number-driven framework, you have two types of values to sell. One type is restorative, beefing up your customers' values that are insufficient due to unnecessarily excessive costs or correctible problems in their productivity. The second type is opportunistic, enabling your customers to seize sales opportunities that would otherwise remain beyond their reach or increase their opportunity to earn higher margins on their current sales.

In tomorrow's competition, remedial values that are proposed to correct deep-seated, long-standing customer problems may be ineffectual. They may be too little or too late to bring a customer back to competitive parity, let along bring him up to

where he can command a competitive advantage. You will therefore have to put your emphasis on preventive values that can
keep your customers from getting into trouble in the first place.
Prevention, not therapy, will have to be your major contribution
to keeping customer cost generators in line while your contribution to customer revenue generators will have to be to make sure
that no market opportunities go by the boards.

Few customers can afford even the temporary disadvantage
caused by unnecessary operations costs or by the opportunity
costs of failing to fully commercialize a market opening. Failures
that are not prevented or opportunities that are not taken on the
rise will have to be amended after the fact. That will be expensive.
Furthermore, there is never a guarantee that a remedy will work.
Even if it does, it may be too far behind the beat for a customer to
regain competitive advantage in a race against faster-moving
competitors.

Your contribution to customer growth will be tomorrow's
main criterion of satisfaction. It will come to be regarded as your
"output," the economic value of what you produce as a business.
But you will have to be more than a good value-adder. You will
also have to be cost-effective at it in order to stay in competition.

If you are a manufacturer, how many tons of particulate
matter do your factories throw into the environment for each
marketable product unit they turn out? The answer may decide
whether or not your factories are competitively affordable. If you
run a hospital, how many patients who come to your critical care
facility become "recalls," having to return because they were
poorly remedied? Your answer may decide whether or not your
critical care service is competitively affordable, especially if tomorrow's social policy decrees that hospitals with the best records
will receive the highest reimbursements.

The value-based purchasing systems of tomorrow are creating a financial incentive for suppliers to produce guaranteed
positive outcomes that improve customer profits. Customers have
an obvious interest in guaranteed outcomes. Suppliers are learning to share their interest, realizing that it is preferable to fulfill
guarantees from the cash flows of a customer's operations than
from their own reserves.

In the health care industry and others, outcomes are being

classified by customers and their suppliers according to outcome groups that rank customer problems by their risk. Three "Solutions Outcome Groups" (SOGs), can be created for any industry:

1. SOG 1 for low risk in fulfilling a high-side guarantee
2. SOG 2 for moderate risk in fulfilling a high-side guarantee
3. SOG 3 for high risk in fulfilling a high-side guarantee

In each case, risk is determined by a supplier's norms for solving problems of similar severity for similar customers. Where the risk is low that a supplier's norms will go unmet, the supplier can guarantee a positive outcome on the high side of the norms. A high risk of meeting high-end norms due to a problem's severity justifies a guarantee on the low side of the norms.

Under a SOG system, it costs everybody less to produce a positive outcome under guarantee. The customer receives the improved profits he expects. His supplier earns full margins that are undiscounted by penalty payments.

Concentrating on the "Disproportionate Contributors"

In order to be competitive, a customer must be able to control his major cost contributors and exploit his major revenue generators. For you to be competitive as a supply partner, you must be able to add significant values to each of them. If your values lack significance and fall on the peripheries of your customers' competitive needs, your partnerability will become peripheral as well.

Customer cost contributors and revenue generators are unequal in their ability to contribute to customer value. Some lines of business earn hundreds of times more profits than others, and many of these contribute low value, no value, or even negative value. High-value businesses are always few, and less than 20 percent of all the profit centers in a company typically contribute as much as 80 percent of its earnings. The same disparity is true for the negative contributors of a customer's cost centers.

The small number of each customer's disproportionately high contributors to costs and earnings must become your premier targets for adding value. Any significant percent of cost that you can help the manager of each critical cost contributor to avoid or reduce will have an exaggerated impact on total customer costs because he is already a high cost contributor. A similar percent reduction in a smaller cost center would have remarkably less impact. In the same way, a customer's major revenue generators must be your premier targets for adding value. Any significant percent of revenues that you can help the manager of each critical profit center make or save will have an exaggerated impact on total customer income.

By concentrating on the disproportionate contributors to a customer, both to his costs and his profitable revenues, you can help him achieve his own competitive objectives. He will already have targeted his disproportionate cost and profit centers as his chief value adders. The majority of his funds are already allocated to flow to them. He knows how important they are. If you, as well, know how important they are to him and how you can help them contribute even more value, he may feel compelled to invite you to make a proposal: How much value can you add compared to how much he must invest with you to achieve it?

Three customer business functions that are often disproportionate cost contributors are good examples of how you can compete on value. Forecasting is one of them. It can add unnecessarily to a customer's cost of doing business if it predicts sales of products that remain unrealized, adding to the costs of inventory, warehousing, insurance, handling, and security, and tying up money that would otherwise have become receivables. At the other extreme, underforecasting can cause stockouts of best-selling products for which a customer has already invested significant funds in advertising and selling. Because these costs cannot be recaptured in sales and the opportunity costs incurred by unfulfilled demand are large, mismanaged forecasting is a major contributor to cost.

Inventory management can be another disproportionate cost contributor. Overstock and stockout problems may originate in forecasting. Or they may come about as a result of an improper manufacturing mix. If inventory is out of keeping with demand, a customer's order fill rate can be negatively affected. Shipments that cannot be made cannot be billed, nor can they contribute to customer satisfaction. If they cannot be billed, they cannot be collected. If they cannot be collected, they cannot contribute to cash flow. Your customer's customers who have been badly served may never call again. An entire future flow of follow-on sales may be lost by a single failure to be timely.

A third disproportionate cost contributor can be receivables collection. Money given up through unnecessarily prolonged collection cycles can be a significant opportunity cost whose value is lost forever even though the outstanding sums may eventually be collected in full. Each day of delay imposes added cost. Because receivables represent the return on money already invested to earn them—in R&D, manufacturing, engineering, and marketing—failure to recover them on time may deprive a customer of the internally generated cash flow to self-finance his next cycle of production and sales.

Identifying Your Proprietary Value Arena

If you can help a customer make his forecasting, inventory, and collection functions more valuable to him, you can help him compete more advantageously. These three functions, which are closely interconnected, affect the costs and cash flows of an entire business. Because you will be laying your reputation on the line every time you propose to add new value to any one of these functions, you must pick your spots carefully. The credibility of your value adding capability is always at risk. To protect it, you must look for customer problems and opportunities that fit your experience. This is your value arena, your "main street" where you are comfortable prescribing solutions that turn out to be right because you know reflexively what is wrong as soon as you see it. Will a problem yield to your solution? Why not? You must be able to say. It always has yielded to it before.

What is your proprietary value arena? Is it your customers' manufacturing, marketing, R&D, data processing or telecommunications, distribution, or office management? Is it their order entry, process scheduling, product design, quality control, inventory management, or receivables collection? What is the nature of the leverage you exert on it? Does it come from doing something faster or better or more cost-effectively or with greater certainty?

What are you very good at—what will you be able to do inside a customer's business that has a predictable effect on his competitiveness? Do you have an experience curve to show for it? Can your customers and you make money on it? Does anybody do it better? If not, you can be its standard-bearer and command a price commensurate with your superior value.

Pricing on value is not a lost art. It is an art that has never been found by most managers because few of them know the value of what they sell. Even fewer know how to charge for it. In computer systems, for example, managers ask: Should we base our prices on the cost of the hardware, the software, or our applications services; on our averaged cost; on our combined cost; or on the cost of the application since hardware and software are often commodities and therefore necessary evils? Others ask: Should we base price on service and applications software since they bring the highest profits? Digital Equipment Corporation uses a formula in which price is composed of the standard book price for hardware and software, time and materials pricing for customized elements, and "some value pricing." This turns out to be mostly a guess since DEC, like almost all of its competitors, rarely knows the value its customers derive from using its systems. If it did, DEC might throw away its price book with its lists of standard charges, throw in the hardware, software, and customized elements for free, and charge in proportion to the net value of the customer costs it can reduce or the revenues it can help to expand.

Under such a value-based pricing regime, DEC's price would be an investment, and the customer's value would be his rate of return on it.

Your value is easy for customers to calculate. It can be the incremental dollars that can accrue to one of their new products when it is able to enter its market sooner than its business plan proposes or reach break-even sooner. Or it can be the incremental dollars that can accrue to the established business of a customer when he is able to maintain its margins longer at maturity or turn it around faster to become rebranded.

Whatever businesses or functions you affect in a customer's operations, tomorrow's major qualifying question will ask whether you affect the *most critical factors*. This is where the money is. With a customer's new product, do you make sure the product is being driven from the outset by its most likely market? With a customer's growth business, can you help fulfill more of its total market opportunity by helping it avoid opportunity loss caused by leaving additional attainable profits on the table? In maturity, can you make small but significant renovations in a customer's product line or promotion strategy or distribution channels that can help maintain its margins?

It will not be sufficient to say, Yes—we can do these things. You must be able to say, "We do these things *best.*" Only then can you become the *industry standard of value* for helping customer startups accelerate their early growth, or customer businesses that are already growing keep growing, or mature businesses turn around at a faster rate.

Norming Your Values

There are three specifications by which you will be judged as a value-adder:

1. Can you meet or exceed the minimum amount of new profits that is regarded as significant by customers in answer to their question, *How much* value will be contributed?
2. Can you meet or come in ahead of the "patient time" that is regarded as maximum by customers in answer to their question, *How soon* will our value begin to flow?
3. Can you meet or exceed the minimum level of assurance that is regarded as necessary by customers in answer to their question, *How sure* can we be that we will realize your proposed value?

Your growth values will rarely meet the high end of all three specifications. Incremental new profits that meet or exceed a customer's minimum requirements may not be deliverable within the maximum amount of time he can afford to wait for them. The larger the profits, the longer they will probably take and the less certain they will be. Major profit improvement, short time frames, and a high degree of certainty coexist more on customer wish lists than in the real world. In instances where large amounts of profits are required, customers must generally wait longer to be grown. But in the majority of situations, the most desirable combination to propose is soonness and certainty. This coupling best serves the customer's interest in maximizing the time value of money by putting smaller sums to work quickly so that they can be grown fast.

In your delivery of growth values, speed and reliability almost always count more than volume. They are a credible pair because they are naturally compatible. Repeated small infusions of new profits, delivered to a customer in quick succession, are generally preferable to the promise of a one-time bonanza. They can be counted on. A customer can put them to work without disruption and he can look forward to more.

The values that you can normally add to your customers can be expressed in an averaged form as *norms*. They will be your most powerful selling tools. With reference to them, you can say, "Normally we are able to help companies that sell your type of products to markets like yours increase their revenues by 25 percent." Or you can say, "Normally we are able to decrease the sales cycle of companies in your industry by one-third, or decrease downtime for manufacturers of consumer appliances like yours by 5 percent within 90 days, or increase their order fill rate by 33 percent over six months, or achieve payback on their investments with us to obtain these benefits within seven to ten months."

What is the current value, you can ask a manufacturing customer, of your inventory's contribution to profits? If you are overstocked according to our norms, or stocked with the wrong mix of goods, or do not accurately know your stock on hand, then your inventory manager is submaximizing his contribution to profits. When you compare your inventory's current performance as a profit contributor to our performance norms, you will see that our norms will enable your manager to maximize his profit contribution by an additional 30 percent.

The dollar difference between your norms for the profit contribution from inventory management and the customer's current contribution will equal your potential value as his partner in the management of his inventory function. It will be your qualifier to be "partner material."

What is the current value, you can ask a supermarket chain customer, of your dry cereal category manager's contribution to profits? If it is submaximum according to our norms, his contribution to your profits is lower than necessary. When you compare your category manager's current performance as a profit contributor to our performance norms, you will see that he can maximize his contribution by another 10 to 12 percent.

Whenever your norms are superior to a customer's current values, you will have found a qualified prospect for improved competitiveness. You will have uncovered a need in the form of a value deficit. This is not the same as a need for a computer, for example, or for a risk management system or for a telemarketing department. It is a need to rejuvenate a value, to repair and replenish it so that it no longer creates a competitive disadvantage for your customer.

Whatever you make, you will have to sell it from your norms. Otherwise, your customers will be unable to forecast the added value that you represent. The only thing they will be able to do is to forecast your added contribution to their costs. Because costs are negative values, customers will require you to minimize them at the outset by discounting your prices and to justify the remainder. Instead of being able to support your margins by relating them to a customer's added values, you will only be able to apologize for the costs you add by lowering them. Each time you do, you will be giving away a share of your own competitive advantage.

Challenging Customers to Become Advantaged

Your normal values are your real products. They enable each customer to predict what will most likely happen to the contribution one of his business functions or lines of business can make to his profits if he allows you to affect it. How much value will it add? When will it add the value? When will the investment be repaid? How sure of all these things can he be?

Each customer whose competitveness you improve will be-

come a contributor to your norms. A poor job lowers your norms.
Superior performances add to the high end of your norms,
perhaps even extending it to an all-time high. The safe way to
compete on value is to use the range of your norms as bookends
and to try to bisect them with each proposal. The leadership way
is to keep pushing out against the high end. A sales scenario
based on norms will have four steps:

1. *The norm challenge.* Dare a customer to compare his current
   performance against your norm.
2. *The significant deviation.* After comparing, the customer
   discovers your norm to be superior, arousing "norm
   envy" of the opportunity to increase his competitive advantage.
3. *The anxiety of deprivation.* With his need aroused, the
   customer calculates the added value of approaching your
   norm.
4. *The request for proposal.* Fortified by his calculations, the
   customer asks for a specific quotation of how much added
   value you can propose, how soon it will accrue to him,
   what his investment will have to be to obtain it, when it
   will be paid back, and what rate of return it will most
   likely yield.

In tomorrow's competition, norm wars will replace price and
performance wars. In norm wars, competitive suppliers will engage each other in a "Strategic Value Initiative." Each competitor
will show his norms at the door as his ticket of admission to a
customer's selection process. The norms will act as his creden-
tials: They will quantify his value and qualify him as experienced
and reliable at adding value to the operations he can affect in the
customer's industry. Unlike the performance specifications of his
products, the performance of his norms will be reflected in the
language of each customer's business—the language of improved
contributions to competitive advantage.

Norms will act as each supplier's positioning statement. They
will position him as either the competitive leader in adding value
to his customers or as an also-ran. If he is the leading value-
adder, his competitors will have to match his achievements or

lower the price they can claim for their second-best values. "Beat me or see your margins beaten down" will become the norm leader's challenge to his competition.

By "leading with your norms," you challenge a customer in three ways:

1. These are our norms for the dollar values of the costs that this business function of yours should be contributing to your total costs—or for the dollar values of the revenues that this business line of yours should be contributing to your total revenues. How do your costs and revenues compare with them?

2. What is the added dollar value that can be contributed to your business function or line of business for each single percentage point by which we can help you more closely approach our norms?

3. What is the competitive advantage this amount of improved contribution will yield to your business—in helping to make it either a lower-cost producer or a greater market shareholder?

By challenging each of your customers to match up his norms with your norms so as to compare his current performance with your standards, each of you will begin the process of partnering in the operations by which he makes and markets his products and services. These are things that customers know a great deal about. Once you free them from having to evaluate your products against those of your competitors and encourage them to analyze the cost-benefits of their processes or products against those of their own competitors, you can help them gain greater control of managing their businesses. This is the supreme form your added value can take.

What are you measured by? You will have to become accustomed to asking your customers' managers. Is it the annual percentage rate of your business growth? Managers in your industry with whom we work normally average an annual gain of 5 to 7 percent. Is it on your trial-to-repurchase ratio? Our norm is a 50 to 60 percent conversion rate. Is it the percent of orders filled on time? Our norm is 90 to 95 percent. Is it receivables collection? Our norm is thirty days. Is it inventory turns? Our annual norm in your business is five to seven. Is it the ratio of revenue to investment? Our norm is three to one.

Guaranteeing Your Value

Your value is the contribution you make to your customers' profits. The worth of every one of your managers, your products, and your services must be measured by the profits they add to your customers. If you are going to be competitive in tomorrow's marketplace, you will have to be a preeminent supplier of the values that can help your customers be more competitive in their own markets.

Adding Values to Consumer Packaged-Goods Customers

If your competitive position is based on the value you add to brand managers of consumer packaged goods businesses, you must help them become more competitive in one or more of their business objectives, such as:

○ Meet volume goals.
○ Meet margin targets.
○ Achieve market share.
○ Reach payback for new products on plan.
○ Maximize the conversion rate of first-time tryers into re-peat purchasers.
○ Maximize the return on promotional investments.
○ Maximize the number of orders filled on time.
○ Minimize unit sales cost.

Metaphor Computer Systems is a company that is good at making consumer brand managers more competitive. Metaphor helps improve their profitable revenues. When it first went to market, it was asking an entry fee of about $1 million for its "grey box and software" system based on narrative claims that brand managers' productivity would be increased and they would be able to interpret supermarket scanner data and warehouse shipment information on their products in hours instead of days. With their decisions supported by data, they would presumably be able to make "more better decisions faster." What impact this might have on profitable sales was left to each manager's imagination.

By the late 1980s, Metaphor had switched to competing on the value of its ability to empower brand managers to reallocate their promotional funds opportunistically from region to region, correlate inventory with their promotions to make sure they had sufficient stock on hand to support their couponing or cents-off offers, and find out fast how much it was costing them when competitors were trying to destabilize their market shares.

In the manner of tomorrow's competitors, Metaphor can show a brand manager how analyzing his couponing effectiveness by region can help him earn an additional $3 to $5 million on each promotion, according to its norms. In another application, Metaphor can show a $2.4 million norm from being able to concentrate trade allowances on a brand manager's best-performing accounts in each region rather than scattershoot them all over the map.

When Metaphor's prospective customers add up the average $3.2 million investment they will make with Metaphor over a two- to three-year time frame, they have normal values to compare it against. As a stand-alone price, $3.2 million may be perceived as expensive in comparison to competitive decision-support systems. But as an investment to yield a normal return of between $6 and $8 million over twenty-four to thirty-six months, the resulting rate of return meets or exceeds customer hurdle rates throughout the consumer packaged-goods industry.

As far as the customers of brand managers are concerned, end-user consumers are becoming consumed by value just as they are predominantly concerned with consuming it. In packaged goods, the nutritional values on the back of the box are more important than the advertising puffery on the face. Information values will increasingly accompany consumer products of all kinds, helping users to maximize their satisfaction. Recipes are an example of application values that will become more important to customer satisfaction than many of the products they accompany. Indeed, foods and beverages will increasingly be regarded as an adjunct to their recipes for good health rather than the traditional other way around.

Adding Values to Industrial Manufacturing Customers

If your competitive position is based on the value you add to manufacturing managers of industrial businesses, you must help them become more competitive in a different set of business objectives such as:

○ Maximize uptime and minimize downtime.
○ Maximize on-spec production as close as possible to zero defects in order to minimize reject rate.
○ Minimize the cost contributions of labor, materials, and energy.
○ Minimize changeover cycles.
○ Minimize life cycle costs of ownership.

If you market computer-aided software engineering systems to manufacturing-based customers, you will have to beat the technical standards of Hewlett-Packard if you want to remain competitive tomorrow. HP sells on the basis of such normal values as these:

○ An average of 185 man-months spent to design a new product from scratch compared with the industry average of 292
○ An average of $300,000 in annual maintenance costs compared with the industry average of $1.3 million
○ An average of eight months for project payback compared with the industry average of fifteen months
○ An average of a 111 percent internal rate of project return compared with the industry average of 81 percent

Hewlett-Packard is also prepared to challenge managers of $10 million plants with additional norms of its value:

○ For each 20 percent reduction in inventory, an average of $60,000 in profits

○ For each 20 percent increase in plant yield, a reduction of material purchases by an average of $640,000

It will be a short step from being able to quantify your normal values to guaranteeing your ability to deliver them, at least at the conservative low end of their range. Tomorrow's customers will demand guaranteed values. They will not be able to plan to maximize their competitiveness without known values because each customer manager will be required to guarantee his or her performance objectives in order to get plans accepted and stake a claim on corporate funds. Guaranteed values will become a part of each company's total quality commitment as a price of partnership. If you fail to help your partner make his commitment, you will fail along with him. For this reason, guaranteeing your values will make it highly likely that you will deliver them. Both you and your customer partners will have too much at risk to permit any deviations from your joint plans. As never before, customers will have call on the commitment of their suppliers just as suppliers will have call on the support of their customers.

When you guarantee your value, you implicitly put your customers to work for you to make sure that you succeed. This is simple self-preservation, not philanthropy. It enables you to influence the ways in which customers implement your products and services, how they manage the projects in which they are applied, how their people are trained—even recruited, motivated, and managed—and how each project's value is measured. In these areas, tomorrow's suppliers will have carte blanche to reach deeply into customer operations and co-manage them with their customer managers or act as outsourcers of some or all of them. As a result, these will become the new capabilities for "selling." If you cannot manage or co-manage the customer operations you affect, you will not be able to guarantee your value. If you cannot guarantee your value, you will not be able to be a co-manager.

When you take inventory of the skill sets that are required for you to be a competitor on value, you must be sure to include assays in the following categories:

○ How good are you in project management? Do you know how to plan a project, how to bring it home on time and on budget, and how to measure its results?

○ How good are you in measuring the delivery of your values on a milestone-by-milestone basis according to plan? Are you as good at measuring as you are in manufacturing?
○ How good are you in training customer people to implement and measure the value of your products, services, and systems?

What would it take for you to become the industry standard of value for your customers in each of these categories? Your answer should become part of tomorrow's strategic plan.

Many companies are still perpetuating the old-style guarantees of the 1980s, guaranteeing the performance of their products or services. Others, like Xerox, guarantee customer satisfaction with their equipment: "If you're not satisfied with your Xerox equipment, we'll replace it." Under their Total Satisfaction Guarantee, Xerox will substitute an identical model or a machine with comparable features and capabilities. Meanwhile, the customer still sustains the opportunity loss of the contribution to his value that the original equipment was planned to make but that is gone forever and can never be made up. In tomorrow's marketplace, Xerox will have to upgrade its guarantee from simply replacing defective machines to replacing lost customer profits if it wants to remain competitive and keep its customers competitive along with it.

Ruling out Debate on Merits

There will be a single test for tomorrow's market dominance. You will be dominant if the values you can add to your customers are accepted as their industry standards of performance. Can you offer them the lowest cost contributed by one of their critical operations? Can you offer them the highest revenues contributed by one of their critical product lines? If so, you can become their dominant supplier because you own the dominant standard that they want to possess for themselves.

Dominant standards of value are money standards. They are a customer's sum total of your product performance values, application values, service values, and training values. They measure the competitive advantage you represent to your customers, which is the principal source of your customer satisfaction. If you can make the highest impact or the soonest, as well as the surest, your impact can become the standard. No one who falls below it, or who cannot prove that he does not, will be able to compete against your standard. Nor can anyone compete with you even if he can exceed your standard but cannot prove it.

Whoever owns the industry standard of value for the customer business functions or lines of business that you affect will be the one to beat. Owning the standard means that no one else can reliably further lower a customer cost or further raise a business line's contribution to customer profits. It also means that no one knows more about how to add value to these customer functions or product lines. By owning a customer industry's standard of value, you also own its standard of knowledge.

When you become their standard of knowledge, customers will turn to you first for competitive information on the two most important things they need to know: *How do they compare to your standard?* If they fall short, *how can they come closer to your standard* by being more cost-free, more productive, or more cash-rich?

If you can help your customers improve the profit contribution of their operations that you affect, the competitive advantage you can confer on them is to help them become the industry standards of value in their own businesses. The competitive advantage that you can confer on yourself will be to ensure your margins. Competing on value rather than on price-performance insulates you against price bargaining. If you fall into discounting, you quickly become countercompetitive. You negate the worth of your business as well as the worth of your products and services. Markets pick up on this right away. When Hewlett-Packard cut the prices of its Vectra line of personal computers up to 22 percent "to strengthen our position in the personal computer market," its position in the stock market dropped overnight by $1.125 a share.

Markets react to where you place your value as well as to how much worth you assign it. As Apple Computer matured as a product-oriented company in keeping with its technology-driven genetic code, it continued to invest all of its value in its computers. This worked well when they were new and unique.

In those days, Apple's business plans could get away with focusing on selling a relatively small number of premium-priced machines to technical buyers and generating sufficient growth. But by the 1990s, other computers had matched many of the Macintosh's user-friendly features. Apple's high-priced-machine strategy had to give way to "aggressive pricing" of new, low-end models that could develop a greater market share at much-reduced profit margins. Once the value had gone out of the boxes, Apple had not planned anywhere else to invest it.

In 1990, Apple aggressively reduced prices on its newest line of Macintosh machines, ending up for the first time in its history with a high-volume, low-price product mix: "A major transformation that changes the way we do business," Apple announced. But the profit consequences were swift and severe. According to Joseph Graziano, Apple's chief financial officer, Apple was caught unprepared. "I'm a little surprised," he said. "We had plans to convert the company from a high-gross-margin company to a low-gross-margin company a little bit differently." Apple still had the operating costs of a low-volume business that was supported by high margins. In addition, the costs of achieving a 20 percent market share came due a lot faster than Apple had calculated, and they were a good deal higher. One of the highest costs was the loss of the jobs of almost 2,000 people.

As a value standard-bearer, you make it difficult for competitors to attack you. When they try to engage you in a debate on product performance merits, they will find that your customers are engaged with you in an entirely different debate. How, your customers will want to know, can we improve the competitiveness of our operations? A competitor's price-performance specifications play only a contributory role, and generally a minor one, in this debate. What counts most is your knowledge of customer operations and how to invigorate their contribution to profits. If you set the standard, that means you can do something no one else can do or do as well or as quickly or with the same degree of certainty. The need for a number 2 or especially a number 3 source of lesser values will be small to nonexistent.

Measuring Value by Customer Satisfaction

Customer satisfaction becomes your "ultimate product" when you compete on value. In turn, value becomes the prime cause of your customer satisfaction. When John Akers, chairman of IBM, says that "we measure all IBMers on their contribution to customer satisfaction," he is saying that they are measured by IBM according to the customer values they add—the same way they are measured by their customers.

In value terms, a "satisfied customer" is one who is receiving the added value he needs on a JIT basis, just in time when he needs it, not simply added products or services. A "satisfactory supplier" is one who is providing the added value according to one or both of two strategies:

1. The supplier is making or saving more money for his customer than the customer can contribute to his own business by himself or in partnership with a competitive supplier at comparable levels of investment and risk.
2. The supplier is costing the minimum amount for his customer by minimizing hidden costs, indirect costs, recurrent life-cycle costs, and all expenditures that the customer must budget as unrecoverable costs instead of returnable investments.

Customer satisfaction comes from adding value to the critical success functions of customer businesses. Within each business, a customer depends on a small number of factors, his "must list." Unless their contribution to his profits can be maximized, he risks competitive disadvantage. The way he typically looks at them, some of the factors on his "must list" will be related to your product, and others will be related to your services. Altogether, seven of them are almost always on every customer's list:

Product-Related Values	*Service-Related Values*
1. Value-to-price relationship	1. Training
2. Product quality	2. Warranty
3. Product benefits and features	3. Repair and replacement
4. Reliability	

The "must list" you receive from any individual customer will depend on "who you ask and how you ask it." If you have an outdated product or process heritage, you will most likely ask the customer people you have come to know best—purchasing managers and their technical functionaries. Your dialogue will concern customer satisfaction in exactly the same ways that it concerns how you sell, focusing on product features and benefits, price, terms, deals and discounts, delivery, and service. If you do this with enough customers, you will come up the same way that 3M has, with more than seventy distinct dimensions of satisfaction in which "product-dominated values are tops." This will encourage you to remain product-driven for another generation while the customer managers above the purchasing and functionary levels, cost center and profit center managers who live or die on business values, will find compelling reasons to do business with competitive adders of customer-dominated values.

If you imitate 3M and allocate your version of seventy dimensions of satisfaction across large numbers of products and service businesses, tomorrow may never come for you. You will be replicating yesterday by ignoring the 80-20 rule that only a critical few dimensions determine 80 percent of satisfaction and that only a small number of your businesses compose the disproportionate growth contributors. You will also be ignoring the growth injunction that says you must know your value, sell your value, and measure the financial values you add so that you can take a dollarized norm challenge to your markets and win against your product-dominated competitors.

7

Competing Cooperatively

Tomorrow's competition will be largely cooperative competition. Suppliers will cooperate with customers to plan their joint growth and co-manage customer facilities and business categories on their customers' behalf. Similarly, suppliers will have to ally with each other to achieve critical masses of skills and resources through various forms of growth partnerships and joint ventures. Inside every company, growth teams will practice cooperative goal setting, participative strategy making, and shared rewards in order to achieve outperformance. For breakthrough projects and major types of campaigns, coalitions of multiple growth teams will be required to bring sufficiently comprehensive resources, or rare ones, to bear in the proper order of magnitude and at the exactly right moments in time.

As a result, one-on-one competition for significant customer opportunities will become virtually extinct. Alliances will compete, not companies.

It is only a matter of time before all megacompanies will have wide-ranging and broad-based networks of growth partners that include one or two banks; suppliers of key component parts like plastics, metals, and semiconductors; and an array of vertical marketers who add the values of specialized applications to niche customers who are too small or too individualized for megacorps to serve directly.

As adversarial relationships between suppliers and customers are replaced by partnerships, trading blocs will form. Each bloc will be a business in itself. Internationally, blocs will operate out of regional strongholds. The three most important bases will be the United States, Europe, and Japan. Among them, they will control up to 80 percent of global trade as they become positioned to be the super*zaibatsu* of the twenty-first century.

Both globally and domestically, competitors in one category are increasingly finding themselves to be allies in several others. Many suppliers are each other's customers as well as competitors for other customers. Many customers compete against their suppliers as members of competitive marketing alliances. A source of supply in one instance becomes a source of demand in another. Some companies are members of so many alliances that they have had to accept competition among them in some categories or markets or regions of the world for the sake of achieving leadership in others.

The proliferation of extended families of customers, suppliers, distributors, and competitors in sausagelike value chains is coming to be known as an "extended enterprise environment."

Cooperating competitors will be looking for the same benefit from each other: the ability to contribute compelling customer growth. *Contribution* will be the key concept in every cooperative business relationship. The reflexive answers to tomorrow's question, How can we compete? is not, Who is our competitor? but Who is our growth partner, who is our joint venturer, who is our strategic ally? No company will be able to succeed without resolving these issues. Without bloc support, big-league competitiveness will be impossible.

Competition is increasingly being waged between collaboratives, confederacies, and coalitions that combine the resources of several companies that have come together in a common cause to compete against other collaboratives whose members have combined for the same reasons.

By the year 2000, there will still be a handful of independent automobile manufacturers, but the mass market in every country will be controlled by no more than seven multinational cooperatives:

1. General Motors-Toyota-Isuzu-Suzuki-Saab-Daewoo
2. Ford-Mazda-Jaguar-Kia
3. Volkswagen-Porsche
4. Chrysler-Mitsubishi-Daimler Benz-Hyundai
5. Fiat-Nissan-Subaru
6. Honda-Rover
7. Peugeot-Citroen-Renault-Volvo

Being partnerable with strategic allies will be a prime requisite for your managers. Only the best growth partners can help ensure their own growth. Relationships with second-best customers or suppliers will virtually guarantee second-best competitiveness. Tomorrow's competitors will be known for the partners they cooperate with and that choose to cooperate with them. In your role as supplier, your self-interest requires you to keep your customer partners strong and in a high-growth mode. As a customer, you have to make sure that you are also growing your suppliers. Every company will accordingly be "growing for three"—itself, its customers, and its suppliers.

Wal-Mart is an example of a company that grows for three. Each of its major trading partners is enrolled in Wal-Mart's "Quick Response" program, which integrates them with the retailer's entire product distribution cycle. The program transmits real-time sales information over a satellite link so that sales are tracked out of inventory at both ends, new orders are automatically placed and invoiced, and each shipment is specifically allocated in time and place to its distribution center and then on to individual stores. In its partnership with Procter & Gamble, Wal-Mart uses Quick Response to maintain low inventories while still keeping its shelves stocked with big-moving P&G products like Pampers diapers that meet its customers' needs. P&G's challenge is to ensure that its customer satisfaction ranking remains high by maintaining on-time deliveries at a virtual 100 percent level.

Allying for Co-Competition

Supplier-customer and supplier-supplier partnerships are tomorrow's competitive "strategic business units." For most middle-size business on the second tier of their industries, and for many smaller and all larger companies, alliances will be a standard way of life.

Well within the 1980s, industries like retailing, semiconductors, airlines, aircraft, and automobile manufacturing were already underway with a multitude of joint ventures, strategic partnerships, and investments in each others' businesses. Competitive individualism, now that the ethic of "my company can beat your company" has passed, was gradually being replaced by a more communal competitiveness of "us against them" between partnering suppliers and a similar sense of community between suppliers and their customers.

Japan's Toyota Motor Company has taken a leadership role in getting involved with its suppliers so that it can arrive at what it calls "a point of mutual trust" in forming "long-term, stable relationships." Toyota works with its suppliers from the product concept stage all the way through production and shipment, seeking to reduce manufacturing costs by cutting the number of faulty parts to a minimum, reducing waste, and automating operating procedures to reduce labor and save energy. "What we are trying to do," Toyota says, "is to present suppliers with our ideas for solving the biggest problems . . . like quality and delivery."

In tomorrow's competition, it will be common for companies to have multiple alliances. A supplier may ally with several customers to be a dedicated source to each of them. At the same time, he may partner with other suppliers in joint ventures to supplement his product lines, expand his technical or manufacturing capabilities, penetrate new markets, or conduct developmental research. While all these relationships are going on, the same supplier may also become a member of a pan-industry consortium to pool communal resources and finances in order to develop exotic or emergent technologies.

In some industries, alliance will be the name of the game. Three-quarters of all biotechnology companies have an average of three strategic partners who are international pharmaceutical makers. Over 90 percent of drug industry alliances are relationships with biotech research companies.

The alliance between Glaxo Holdings PLC, maker of prescription drugs, and Gilead Sciences, Inc., a biotechnical manufacturer, brings together Glaxo money and an anticancer drug invention. The keys to the relationship are access to development funds for Gilead and access to technology for Glaxo. Alliances like this show how important it has become for megacorps to be able to make new product introductions whether or not they have made their own new product inventions. It also shows that as far as R&D is concerned, megacorps have come to realize that microbusinesses can generally "D" faster as well as "R" more innovatively.

In tomorrow's typical competitive posture, a customer and his partners, allied with his suppliers and their partners, will be operating as teams going up against other similarly multipartnered teams. The right choices for each "partner mix" will be crucial. Each partner will win or lose his bids for team membership based on his ability to maximize a partnership's competitive advantage. Can he contribute the lowest costs, giving his partnership a competitive edge in resourcing? Can he contribute the most marketable products, the most cost-effective applications, or the most productive customer training? If so, his teams may be able to gain an edge in improving their customers' profits.

Under the terms and conditions of cooperative competition, an unpartnered or poorly partnered business—which is a business that is in alliances with other businesses that are themselves poorly partnered—will be noncompetitive.

Becoming a cooperative competitor can be culturally shocking. Meeting two requirements can ease the transition: being a major source of growth for your allies, as they must be for you, and replacing outmoded rivalries with new competitors.

1. *You must be important sources of growth profits to each other.* The contribution of competitive advantage that you can make to a customer or supplier must be significant. Only then will partnering with you be compelling to your partners. To be an important source of their growth means that you must account for worthwhile incremental profits to your common customers. You must be able to deliver them in a timely fashion, recognizing the time value of money. You must also be dependable. Your partners must be able to count on you to improve the profits of your joint

customers when you say you will and by the amounts you promise. Your desirability as a partner will be in direct proportion to your reliability.

2. *You must have the same competitors.* In the old tradition of selling products and services as an alternate vendor, each supplier was only concerned with defeating his own competitors. In tomorrow's competition, you must concentrate on defeating your customer's competitors. Unless you and your allies have this objective in common with your customers, you cannot be partners with them or with each other.

A customer's competitors are constraints on his growth. He has two types of them. One is internal, the sources of his current costs that he must reduce if he is to improve his profits. His second source of competition is external: the sales opportunities for which he competes. If he is going to be able to improve his profits, you must help him increase his margin leadership or his market penetration.

When two companies sit down to plan a partnership, each will have to know how he can grow a common customer's profitability, and by how much and how soon. As a result, partners will be in the business of *enhancing a common customer's business*. This must be true no matter how diversified two partners are or even how disparate in size, life-cycle phase, or culture they may be. At the heart of their relationship will be their knowledge of how to improve customer profits and thereby their own.

Customer-enhancing alliances founded on supplier-supplier partnerships will be based on two principles of tomorrow's competition:

1. *Never make what you can buy.* This is designed to help limit your investments, especially in the ownership of capital-intensive assets such as manufacturing and physical distribution operations. It is also a warning against committing to make and sell hardware that will quickly mature and become obsolete.

2. *Never buy out what you can buy into.* This is designed to help you learn your way into new business opportunities, especially emergent technologies and their market applications, by

making minority investments in them. It is also a reminder to assure the management continuity of founding entrepreneurs in any high-growth business you ally with.

Selecting Your Kind of Co-Competition

There are five basic types of co-competitive organization styles that will play prominent roles in tomorrow's competition: sales and marketing partnerships, manufacturing partnerships, joint ventures, R&D partnerships, and minority investments.

Sales and Marketing Partnerships

In sales and marketing partnerships, a supplier comes together with another supplier or customer to market some or all of their products jointly in what is essentially a market penetration strategy. This enables both partners to receive the benefits of selling a more comprehensive product or service system without the need for either partner to manufacture and market all of its components.

Sales partnerships extend each product line's reach into an existing or new market. From a make-or-buy perspective, it is a "buy" decision by both partners. For the supplier of the product line that is extended, the alternative would be self-manufacture. For the supplier of the market that is entered, the alternative would be marketing, sales, and distribution channel expansion.

MIPS Computer Systems may be one of tomorrow's business models for microcorps that wants to be a giant killer. MIPS has become a multimillion dollar publicly traded company with little capital and no in-house manufacturing capability or distribution. The company decided to be a designer of microchips and a licenser of their production and sales to a group of partners in return for royalty fees. While MIPS makes less money on royalties than it would by making and selling its own chips, it avoids the expense of building and owning fabricating plants and fielding a sales force. At the same time, it assures multiple competitively priced sources of supply.

In line with its low-investment strategy, MIPS also makes

computer workstations for other computer makers to sell as their own brands. This keeps MIPS from competing against its own chip customers and encourages the widespread adoption of its technology.

The airline industry is a network of marketing partners. Using Air France and Lufthansa as a model joint marketing alliance, Swissair and Scandinavian Airlines Systems also coordinate schedules and routes and go even further by sharing 10 percent of each other's stock. Sabena, Belgium's airline, has an alliance with British Airways and KLM Royal Dutch Airlines where each has a 20 percent stake in Sabena. Among commuter airlines, forty-three of the fifty largest regional airlines were operating as affiliates of major carriers in 1990.

In mass retailing, major manufacturers and their retail customers who have the same consumers in common are becoming supplier-customer allies. At Warner-Lambert, the belief is that "to get to the consumer, you have to do it together with the retailer." Procter & Gamble sees it the same way: "The major retailers around the world are moving toward cooperative alliances with a select few suppliers. We must be one of them." The P&G strategy to be "alliance material" is to become "the most desirable supplier to deal with."

In order to achieve desirability, which is its way of being compelling, P&G is asking itself questions like these: How much will it help our retailers if both companies use the same record-keeping number to identify each item, eliminating the need to reticket shipping containers one by one when they arrive? How helpful will it be to ship orders according to a retailer's sales forecasts so that smaller inventories can be maintained? How much will it help if on-time deliveries are increased from 94 percent to 99.6 percent?

IBM keeps adding relationships for jointly marketing information services. Most of them are based on minority investments in small software companies. IBM also uses multiple third-party partnerships with vertical market specialists to penetrate their niche markets.

Alliances between two suppliers may be based on a simple cooperative selling agreement or may take the more complex form of a new corporate enterprise, a third entity whose ownership, funding, and rewards are shared as a joint business venture. Joint agreements can be entered into on a specified short-term basis or they can run indefinitely. They can market a single product or service system or several, including systems of other alliances.

Manufacturing Partnerships

In manufacturing partnerships, two suppliers can come to-gether to manufacture the products of one of them or a new product. This is essentially a form of technology sharing. The automobile industry is a network of manufacturing partnerships. Ford owns 25 percent of Mazda, which makes cars in the United States for Ford. In return, Ford makes compact trucks for Mazda. Each owns a piece of Korea's Kia Motors, which produces Ford cars for export to the United States. Ford and Nissan make each other's cars in Australia while Ford and Volkswagen have merged into a single company in Latin America that exports trucks to the United States.

General Motors has somewhat less than 50 percent owner-ship in Isuzu, which has a joint venture in the United States with Subaru, which is partly owned by Nissan. GM also owns half of Sweden's Saab and half of Korea's Daewoo Motors, which makes Nissan cars for sale in Japan and Pontiacs for the United States. GM and Toyota produce cars for each other in the United States and Australia.

Before partnerships came to dominate the way automobiles are made, manufacturers solicited bids from competing suppliers for precisely defined parts and then went to work beating down their prices. With partnering, one or two suppliers are being selected as strategic growth allies. They are given responsibility for original product design and development as well as inventory control and just-in-time delivery. Up front, they may have the chance to make investments in their joint projects in order to be able to share in the partnership's profits. Their profit shares may act as part or all of their "price."

In aircraft manufacture, the Boeing Company also believes that "it is no longer realistic for us to go it alone." Boeing partners with companies in Japan and Italy, and with other global subcon-tractors to supply parts for its commercial airliners. Three Japanese companies—Mitsubishi, Fuji, and Kawasaki—are Boeing's principal partners.

Joint Ventures

In joint ventures, two partners come together to form an equally held third business. This is essentially a business development strategy. It enables both partners to modernize their existing technologies and, by combining capabilities, commercialize new sciences at half the cost within a potentially compressed time frame.

A joint venture is a new competitive business created by mating two or more existing businesses. Each of the venturing businesses has an equal investment and holds equal equity. The venture they form is separate and apart from either of them, possessing its own management, mission, and capabilities. Joint ventures are usually in the same business or a closely allied, logically extended business of their venturers. Each ally contributes financing and technical and marketing resources. One venturer may contribute advanced technology; he may possess superior engineering or more cost-effective manufacturing skills. The other venturer may contribute advanced marketing; he may have superior market knowledge or selling skills. Still another type of pairing may be based on complementary technologies, two differently based sciences that can have a multiplier effect on the same market when they are joined.

Joint ventures may be formed to modernize a mature technology, create a new technology, or combine efforts to try to produce a scientific breakthrough. Ventures of the future will be dedicated to penetrate complex emergent markets such as the combination of home information and entertainment that joins show business, education, sports, and news skills. These require the hardware and software capabilities of businesses in telecommunications, information processing, news and entertainment, insurance, and banking.

General Motors is a partner with Toyota in a joint automobile venture called NUMMI, New United Motor Manufacturing. The venture is designed to produce General Motors Chevrolet cars using Toyota's advanced automated manufacturing and labor management methods. General Motors is contributing its knowledge of the American car market and its nationwide distribution system to the venture.

A joint venture like NUMMI can become an immediate major player in its industry. It can renew the capabilities of the venturers as each learns from the other, enabling it to modernize its base sciences by technology transfer, diversify its product lines, move into new markets, and adopt new forms of labor relations.

Joint ventures are having an increasing global reach. Two of the world's largest high-technology conglomerates, Daimler-Benz and Mitsubishi, have allied to develop and market new automobile technologies, breakthrough aerospace materials, and innovative microelectronics and to share each other's global distribution channels. A continuous series of mutually undertaken projects involving technology exchange and market access takes place between the venturers. Mitsubishi's main interest in the alliance is in automotive and aerospace businesses. For Daimler-Benz managers, the principal concerns are electronics and space technologies.

Research & Development Partnerships

In research & development partnerships, two suppliers come together to share the risks and rewards of financing and staffing a development opportunity. This is essentially a technology penetration strategy. It enables both partners to take on a leading-edge science and its commercialization without having to be burdened by unaffordable financing.

In the computer industry, joint development is a popular form of alliance. Digital Equipment Corporation and Apple Computer are in agreement to jointly develop products that will connect the two companies' systems, especially Apple's personal computers and DEC's larger minicomputers. This alliance gives Digital an opportunity to penetrate Apple's office desktop market and gives Apple entry into DEC's corporate market. Because IBM has been the historically dominant supplier in both of these markets, it is the alliance's common competitor.

In a similar manner, Microsoft and Ashton-Tate have allied to make new software products to manage databases that run on

huge computer networks. These products compete directly with
IBM software, just as the DEC-Apple alliance competes directly
with IBM hardware. Through their joint venture, Microsoft gains
access to Ashton-Tate's distribution system to medium-size businesses while Ashton-Tate acquires Microsoft's technology for
advanced software.

Each R&D partnership is a scientific "skunk works," an
organizationally outcast group whose mission is to grow leading-
edge technology that neither partner possesses on his own or
could develop or afford to develop independently. The contributing technologies may be extensions of each partner's base
sciences, but the result of the partnership should be a breakthrough that can advance common customer competitiveness.

With an R&D partnership, costs, risks, and rewards are
shared by the partners so that each sponsor can maximize his
resources. As soon as a desired new technology has been developed, the objectives of the partnership are considered to be
achieved.

Minority Investments

In minority investments, one partner invests in the R&D of
another, usually in order to obtain an early toehold in an emergent growth technology. This is essentially a technology insurance strategy. It enables the investing partner to learn a promising technology without having to be in it, to keep his options
open to get in further or get out, and to hedge his bets in a similar
fashion among several competitive new technologies.

Minority investors buy the right to influence a technology's
direction along with securing a first option on its purchase or
use. They also may obtain a position to increase their original
minority stakes all the way up to total ownership.

For a large company, multiple minority investments act as a
form of externally outsourced R&D. New business opportunities
can be explored without funding initial startup costs or making a
full-scale commitment to enter then as an active player. As a
result, minority investments are generally kept to a 20 percent
level of ownership or below. Not only does this help hedge bets
and keep options open, it also permits the evaluation of diverse

approaches while postponing the need to commit to an early decision on which one may be the eventual winner.

Through minority investments, investors acquire catbird seats to learn how a new science must be managed, how its assets and liabilities match up, how it compares with rival sciences, how it must be resourced and financed, what its most likely areas of commercialization may turn out to be and when they are likely to occur, and where the most profitable market opportunities may be found.

General Motors is a model of a modern minority investor. One of GM's partnerships is with Teknowledge, a developer of artificial intelligence "expert systems" that can be used to drive GM's automated assembly functions. General Motors has taken an initial 11 percent stake in Teknowledge, along with a 15 percent investment in Applied Intelligent Systems, another artificial intelligence developer. Similarly, in the field of robotic vision, GM has a 15 percent investment in View Engineering and an 18 percent ownership of Robotic Vision Systems. Teknowledge itself has five partners in addition to General Motors.

Each of these alliances is a form of recognition of tomorrow's competition. It shows that it has become too costly to fail, where the entire enterprise may be put at risk by missing out on a new technological curve or an emergent market opportunity. At the same time, it has also become equally costly and often unaffordable to succeed. Even with success, or as a result of the investment it requires, the next generation of product development for any competitor may be the last.

Testing Partnership Significance

Partnering will be profitable for you, and affordable, only with suppliers and customers that contribute and receive significant competitive advantages from you. Three criteria are useful to test each partnership's significance:

1. *Significance of profit contribution.* A partnership's minimal annual profits must equal or exceed each partner's hurdle rates for return on investments in his own businesses.

2. *Continuity of profit contribution.* A partnership must provide predictable profit flows over a continuous twelve- to
thirty-six-month time frame.
3. *Growth of profit contribution.* A partnership must provide
an increasing annual rate of profit over its commercial life
so that it remains a prime investment option for both
partners.

These three criteria can help you determine whether a candidate for partnership is truly prospective. The gains are in the
form of a continuing stream of new growth profits. The quintessential risk will be failure to achieve accelerated mutual growth,
the compelling reason for the partnership's existence. This will
mean that you have not found common customers to grow. If less
growth is realized than planned, the opportunity represented by
the partners' alliance will have been more or less lost.

Sustaining Alliances

In tomorrow's competition, changing partners will be big news.
The one-night stands of vending, where sales made today have
no predictable bearing on sales that may be made tomorrow, will
be replaced by long-term, ongoing relationships that are under-
written by mutual profitability. The partners will have more to
lose than gain by changing partners. The front-end loaded startup costs of a new relationship will be one deterrent. Another will
be the potential opportunity cost of losing the momentum of
profit-making continuity to take what will inevitably be a gamble
on a new partner—maybe a winning gamble but, then again,
maybe not.

Any inducement to change partners must be based on
greater reliability. Most managers will agree with Carl Reichardt,
chairman of Wells Fargo, who has made it clear that he is "much
more interested in reliability than being on the leading edge."
Reliability will have to be virtually total; being "somewhat more
reliable" will not be sufficient to allay the risk of change.

As a result, the mean time between changes of partners will
be long. It will be easier to become a parallel partner in an

adjacent niched capacity than to displace an established partner already in place or wait for an untimely departnering as a result of his own mismanagement. Long-term strategic alliances will have a built-in immunity to competition that will make them, in effect, consensual monopolies. Their impact on competition for a piece of the partnership's action will be to eliminate it.

For both suppliers and customers, partnerships will prove to be a more cost-effective way of exchanging values than traditional competitiveness. Vendor-style competition, with its wasteful duplication of requests for proposals going out and the reciprocal duplication of sifting through the virtually identical bids that come back, has become too expensive on both sides. Too many man-hours are involved for the modicum of differentiation that is gained.

Vendors have shown their customers that they rarely know enough about customer needs. In turn, customers have shown that they rarely address the real costs of acquiring products and services, which are not simply what they pay for the products or services themselves but also include their life-cycle "costs of ownership" for application, implementation, and education. In buying computers, for example, it has been estimated that it costs customers $100 in training for every $1 they spend on hardware.

The longer that partners work together, the harder it is to pry them apart. The supplier partner will, in many cases, become the custodian of his long-term relationships as customer managers are promoted or transferred or leave. This makes a supplier invaluable over time, if not as the conscience of the customer and the corporate memory of the alliance, then as his profit-making historian and cataloguer of what has worked, what has not worked, and therefore, what may work best for the co-competitors in the future.

8

Competing by Co-Managing

In tomorrow's competition, selling to major customers will be replaced by managing your customers' lines of business or their business functions that you can affect and bundling your products, services, and systems into a management plan. Whereas in the 1980s major-account selling took place under the caveat "*Know* your customer's business," "*Manage* your customer's businesses" will supersede it.

Anyone who puts competitive time and effort into placing his products with the 20 percent of his customers who account for up to 80 percent of his profitable sales will be in the Dark Ages. The competitive edge will be in getting tangent to one of a customer's critical success factors—an operating process or line of business on which his competitive advantage depends—and helping him manage its assets. If you can move up to that point on the value chain, you will be at the nearest point to your customers and the furthest point from what you may once have regarded as the source of your businesses, your manufacturing processes, and their products.

Suppliers who continue to think of manufacturing as their asset base, and think of their products as what they must sell rather than their ability to manage their customers' operations, will fall back to become subsuppliers and subcontractors to their competitors who have made the quantum leap to co-managing.

In order to compete tomorrow, you must face up to one of the most crucial decisions about your business: Can you help your customers manage one of their critical functions or critical lines of business more cost-effectively than they can manage it themselves? Can you help them dominate a category of their market or operate one of their key processes so that its contribution to their costs is reduced or its contribution to their revenues and earnings is increased?

If you can, you will be able to position yourself as a customer facility manager or business category manager. This will free you from selling your products—computers by the box, oil by the barrel, or beer by the case—and once you establish your management value, it can free you from having to sell at all. As a facility manager, you can move your products into your customer operations, integrate them as necessary with a multivendor mix of other products and services, and run the resulting supersystem for its maximum contribution to customer profits.

A computer maker, for example, will no longer simply sell hardware and software products on a unit-by-unit basis or even networked together in systems. Instead, he will provide a completely integrated megasystem composed of the optimal mix of his own products and the products and services of other suppliers, matched for their maximum contribution, and then manage the total system's operation in the most cost-effective manner.

Such a systems integrating company may specialize in managing the inventory and forecasting functions of its customers who make and market multiple products. Or another integrator may manage its customers' billing and collection or telecommunications functions, setting up and operating the systems it has integrated.

A supplier to the health care industry may become a manager of hospital intensive care units or its hospital customers' home care services rather than act merely as a provider of diagnostic or therapeutic products sold to these operations. A manufacturer of corporate aircraft may manage its customers' business fleets instead of competing to sell its airplanes to them. The company will be in a position to integrate its own products and services, as well as other manufacturer's products, and even pilots, mechanics, and insurance services to create the optimal mix of aircraft and maintenance for each customer's needs. Most of the money a facility management company like this makes will come from management fees, one component of which can be a value-based percentage of the customer funds it helps to save or earn.

Facility managers can also act as investment bankers. Electronic Data Systems and Texas Air Corporation have experimented with a model equity-for-business partnership that blends financing, data processing, and strategic business planning. In return for receiving all of Texas Air's business involving information technology, EDS would invest $250 million in Texas's "System One" reservation facility.

Logically Extending Sole-Sourcing

In the 1980s, customers began to get into the process of concentrating their purchases with a small number of "strategic allies." They entered into a renewable, long-term partnership with each of their dedicated suppliers, who typically approached them in this manner:

"As your sole source, we will improve the profit contribution of your operations that we affect under the following conditions: We will need access to their operating managers. We will need access to their data. We will need to share in their strategic business planning process so that we can anticipate your changing requirements and incorporate them into our joint plans." It is only a logical extension from this type of sole-sourcing to managing the customer's entire operation that is being sourced as a way of guaranteeing the maximum improvement of his profits.

Facility management is a general term for taking charge of a customer's business operation and running it for the customer under a management contract. In consumer packaged-goods businesses, running a product's entire category for a retail customer is called category management. In either case, there is one rule above all: *Integrate or be integrated.* Either take leadership to integrate a major customer's facility or category or a major component of it, or you risk becoming integrated into a competitor's management system.

If you become integrated rather than an integrator, the penalties will be severe. You will no longer have the chance to participate in any of the major up-front "What if?" type of policy-making decisions with your customers, who will make them with their integrator. You will be shut out of access to the key sources of information that go into growth decisions. You will also be shut out of access to the customer decision makers themselves. Your customer knowledge will be limited, your customer access carefully controlled, and your competitive position subordinated to the integrator. He will deal with you as a vendor, issuing requests for a proposal like this that will make it impossible for you to be anything but a price-based subcontractor:

> Design a brake set that will stop a 2,200-pound car within 200 feet at 60 miles an hour that can perform a minimum of 10 times in succession without fading more than 10 percent between the first and tenth application. The brake set must fit within a 12-inch housing and weigh a maximum of 2 pounds. The original price must not exceed $40 a set and must be progressively reduced each year by 3 to 7 percent.

When you become the prime outsourcer for the management of a customer facility or category of his business, you and your customer will have three options:

1. The customer can continue to own the facility and you can contract with him to manage it. You can retain all his people or only some of them. As a part of your role as prime contractor, you will integrate his operating system and maintain it at state-of-the-art levels with an optimal mix of the products and services of multivendor subcontractors.

2. The customer can sell you the facility outright and continue to be its customer. You will be able to serve other customers with its resources as well.

3. The customer can spin out the facility and make you a co-

owner in a joint venture that converts the customer's former cost center into a profit center, makes it into a new corporate entity, and serves multiple customers while continuing to serve your own customer. You will be a co-investor with the customer as well as his co-manager.

Outsourcing allows customers to get people off their payrolls; products out of their inventories; cost centers off their balance sheets; and peripheral, highly technical, or rapidly obsolescent facilities out from under their management. For you, it can provide opportunity to penetrate new businesses where your expertise and your products or services play a significant role.

Outsourcing is an acknowledgment by a customer that he has found in you a supplier who can improve the profit contribution of one of his critical business functions or lines of business better than he can. Moving up to facility management says something more: You not only know how to implement your products and services into customer operations but you also know how to apply other suppliers' products and services in combination with your own, integrating them and managing their combined contribution to improve the customer's total business.

Making "Selling" a One-Time Event

Virtually all of tomorrow's companies will have to consider outsourcing many of their clerical, maintenance, and support services. Cost will frequently be the initial driver. A second force will be continuing customer restructuring, which makes many centralized internal cost centers unjustifiable for an ever-smaller, more compact business. But the main reason will be the need for customers to concentrate on their core businesses rather than on their peripheries; as Cummins Engine Company says, "to focus our people on making engines and not running computers." Somebody else who focuses on running computers will always be able to run them better.

The Ford Motor Company-TRW relationship is an example of mutual profit improvement by sole-sourcing. In common with automobile industry standard practice, Ford had previously relied on several suppliers for each of its major components. Multiple sources gave Ford a sense of security. It also gave Ford down-scaled pricing and access to free services as a result of each alternate supplier's attempts to gain and hold Ford business.

In 1987 Ford appointed TRW to design and supply all of Ford's safety components such as seat belts and air bags in North America on renewable five-year cycles. TRW set up a dedicated business unit to serve Ford's requirements. At once, Ford's buying cycle and TRW's sales cycle were condensed. Ford no longer had to pay the costs of issuing multiple requests for proposal and evaluating competitive bids, saving the personnel and real estate expenses set aside to receive them. Ford and TRW also eliminated the added costs to both of them of progressive vendor runoffs. In their place, each gained economies of scale from a one-time single large-volume bid.

For TRW, price has become a once-every-five-years negotiation, netting out somewhere between the value that TRW puts on the certainty of an assured customer and Ford's value of an assured source of predictable quality supply. From the outset of each year, TRW can economize by planning its production and inventory and reduce, expand, or reallocate its sales force and technical support services.

As far as the Ford safety components business is concerned, competition has effectively ended within five-year time frames. The Ford-TRW partnership is exclusive. Other suppliers of safety components will have to find niches to serve on its fringes or become integrated as subsuppliers to TRW.

Like TRW, IBM manages several different levels of outsourcing services, from designing and building customer data centers that it will run to managing integrated customer information systems. Once it has won an outsourcing contract, IBM is in position to influence the purchase of all the hardware and software components that go into the integrated system it structures. When IBM "sells" its own equipment in this integrated way, without actually having to sell it at all, its normal sales cost of up to 20 percent drops to virtually nothing. The psychological cost of one of IBM's worst nightmares—archcompetitor Electronic Data Systems acting as a facility manager with an IBM customer to integrate a system based on archcompetitor Hitachi computers—also drops to zero.

Systems integration projects can be financed the usual way by a customer's capital funds or by external funds from bank loans, leases, or cash that is provided by the integrator himself in the form of equity taken in a system, royalties based on a system's performance, or a takeover of the system and conversion into an outsourced capability under integrator management. When a lease expires, the customer can choose to renew it or buy it back.

Eastman Kodak Company has retained IBM to manage its worldwide data communications facilities. IBM has also built and operates Kodak's corporate data center. At the same time, Kodak has invested $40 million to retain Digital Equipment Corporation to manage its telecommunications operations. As part of both deals, IBM and DEC have bought some of Kodak's assets and employ some former Kodak technical staff. In order to keep its hand in, Kodak still assists in the management of its outsourced facilities but not to the point where it keeps Kodak "from getting on with more strategic operations such as making photographic film and other imaging technologies."

Kodak's IBM-managed data center is also open for business with other companies that do not want to build or maintain large computing infrastructures of their own. In this way, Kodak has converted its computer operations from a cost center to a profit center, getting it off the books as well as getting it off the premises. Whatever revenues Kodak receives from its semispun-out facility will add to its minimum annual savings objective of 15 percent from outsourcing. The main competitive advantage should nonetheless result from the new profits that flow from a superior integration of information to achieve Kodak's strategic business objectives.

Three of the largest national telephone companies have combined in an alliance to plan and manage the internal telecommunications systems of multinational corporations throughout the world. Companies that contract out their telephone network management to British Telecommunications PC, Nippon Telephone & Telegraph Company, and Deutsche Bundepost Telekom can go one-stop shopping at the triumvirate for all their communications needs, from equipment integration to staffing and handling the complexities of international regulations and tariffs.

Facility management on this scale puts the facility manager at the apex of customer control. Electronic Data Systems manages data processing for First Fidelity Bancorporation, integrating the bank's mostly IBM computer systems and operating them as an outsource. In this role, EDS prescribes all equipment upgrades and replacements that go into the systems. Since EDS has a 20 percent minority investment in Hitachi Data Systems, IBM is at risk of either being frozen out of the bank's future business or coming under severe pricing leverage in order to compete against Hitachi.

People skills supersede product performance in the management of a customer's facility. The supplier with the best managers will win. Honeywell's Commercial Buildings Group has set down qualifications like these for its health care facilities managers:

> Work on-site at the client's health care facility, hospital or medical center . . . be responsible for managing the integration of equipment and work processes into a Total Systems Approach that functions hand-in-hand with the operation of the facility. Administrative and technical responsibilities include management of people and finances as well as overseeing the functioning and maintenance of energy/environmental control systems, electrical and mechanical systems, telecommunications systems, biomedical services, and security. Specific duties will involve reducing operating costs by providing necessary recommendations and technical resource management to hospital departments. This position functions in a consultant capacity.

In consumer packaged goods, Philip Morris manages the cigarette category in many major supermarket chains in which Johnson & Johnson acts as category manager for health and beauty aids and Nabisco manages their dry cereals category.

Over time, closely partnered relationships like those managed by Philip Morris, TRW, and IBM tend to become entrenched. With each renewed contract, the partners become more valuable to each other. TRW, for example, has extended its role at Ford beyond manufacturing. It maintains Ford's inventory, correlates its own research and product development with Ford's needs, and designs its products to integrate with Ford's automotive design directions. Ford, for its part, shares proprietary market research findings with TRW, makes sure that they are driven into TRW's product designs, and acts as a consultant to TRW's technology and cost control managers. All of these activities are governed by a joint Ford-TRW business plan.

Trading on Your Project Management Skills

Tomorrow's customer challenges will no longer be directed to your R&D or engineering or manufacturing capabilities that can answer the question, How good is your product? or How reliable is your delivery? Nor will they be directed to your sales and marketing capabilities that can answer, How much are your discounts or merchandise payments or extra allowances of free goods? or How much free service or technical support do you provide? Tomorrow's pressures will be on your ability to integrate all the cost contributors and revenue generators in a customer's process or department and manage them for maximum profitability.

Tomorrow's questions will ask, How much do you know about this function of my business? How good are you at integrating its component parts and systems? and How much more of a profit contribution will you enable it to make that will exceed what anybody else can do or what I can do myself . . . in short, *are you the best manager of this part of my business?* If you are, a customer will be compelled to place it in your hands. You will be more than his preferred vendor or sole source of supply. You will be his co-manager.

When you co-manage, you must trade on your project management capabilities rather than your product features and benefits or price-performance ratios. The fact that you are Johnson & Johnson and make Band-Aid brands gives you "proposal rights" as a co-manager for Band-Aid's category of health and beauty aids (HBA), but it will take more than Band-Aids to get you the job of outsourcing profits for the HBA category as a whole. The same applies to Nabisco. No matter how high the unit margins are on its Shredded Wheat brand, managing the dry cereals category for its supermarket customers requires a profit-improvement planogram and business case for the entire cereals category that will maximize its total contribution to each customer chain.

In co-managing customer facilities where sales are made without selling, your sales process will undergo change. The consultative concept of the caring and capable "customer's man" will have to replace the wolf-pack strategy of companies like Cincinnati Milacron where the sales force is assigned to "go out to kill" competitors instead of grow customers. Another relic will be the "attack manager," the sales warrior who is always ready "to bite the head off a chicken" and, along with him, the hunter-skinner approach to selling where hunters track down leads and skinners follow up by stripping customers of their money. The entire concept of the customer's money will be revised. Instead of believing that "my job is to put my hand in the customer's pocket and take his money," you will have to reposition your sales function to put its hands into customer pockets to add new money that customers can share with you as your reward for contributing to their growth.

As you evolve from being a competitive product manufacturer or service supplier to a co-managing partner, and as the definition of your product undergoes conceptual change from being some form of hardware or software to become an improvement in customer profits, the specifications of what you sell will be significantly altered. Some of your "specs" as a facility manager will look like this:

○ System acquisition costs saved
○ Life-cycle costs of ownership saved
○ Overhead costs saved
○ Utilities costs saved
○ Manpower costs saved
○ Consumables costs saved
○ Maintenance and service costs saved
○ Revenues or earnings expanded

In each case, you will have to prove to customers exactly where you are a better alternative than their in-house operation or a competitive facility manager. This will be your first hurdle, clearing the customer's current cost barriers and revenue standards by enough of a margin to make you a compelling competitor.

A cost-benefit analysis is the standard method for proving on paper your capability to add value in advance of proving it in actual operation in a customer's business. The analysis shows a customer how much value he can expect to realize in return for his investment with you, when he will be paid back, how the cash flows will accumulate over the investment's useful life, what their total net value will be when they fully accrue, and the rate of return his investment will yield. Cost-benefit analyses like the model shown in Figure 7 are the "spec sheets" of facility management sales.

Your second hurdle of proof will be qualitative. It focuses on two concerns: product or performance quality and service. Can your outsource managers maintain product quality that will equal or exceed each customer's current standards? Can they match the satisfaction requirements that must be met to keep their customers competitive in their industries?

Can they be consistently responsive to their customers' needs, can they meet their customers' internal deadlines and minimize their downtimes, and can they provide backup capabilities that are sufficient to meet each customer's peak conditions and accelerate disaster recovery?

Whether you manage a customer's operating facility or a category of business as his outsourcer, or act as the integrator of one of his systems for a key process, your role as co-manager will be to propose and manage a series of profitable projects. Each project must make its own incremental contribution to the customer's competitive advantage. For this reason, project management skills will be indispensable to you as one of tomorrow's competitors—not only in your own businesses, where they have always been critical success factors, but also inside the businesses of your customers.

Your projected incremental advantages to customer businesses act as an overlay to their strategic business plans. Take out

Figure 7. Cost-benefit analysis.

	Year 0	Year 1	Year 2
1. New equipment investment			
2. Revenue			
3. Cash savings			
4. Noncash expense			
5. Depreciation ACRS			
6. Material trade-in			
7. Profit improvement BIT (3-5+6)			
8. LESS: Income tax (%)			
9. Investment tax credit (10%)			
10. NET PROFIT IMPROVEMENT (7–8+9)			
11. CASH FLOW (1+5+10)			
12. PAYBACK (cumulative cash flow)			
13. Present value (10% factor)			
14. Discounted cash flow (11×13)			
15. NET PRESENT VALUE CASH FLOW (14)			
16. RETURN ON INVESTMENT (10÷1)			

this function and its costs, your project says. Or take out your internal resources from this category and expand its revenues. Here is what your business will look like in each of these scenarios:

Plan A: Your business according to your current three-year plan
vs.
Plan B: Your business overlaid by our project plan over the next three years

Becoming a Quality Co-Manager

Whatever business you are in, when you become a facility manager you become a money manager. The money belongs to your customers. It will be invested with you to obtain the yield you propose from the projects you co-manage in each customer's operations. Your customers will invest their money with you only to make more money. The new money they make will come from reduced costs and expanded top or bottom lines. Your pay will be based on how much you return for every dollar invested with you.

A co-management project starts when a customer accepts the consequence of your asking, What if your competitive advantage can be improved by this much this soon?

If you are proposing to be a facility manager for a manufacturing or processing customer, you must be prepared to prove the enhanced contribution one of his business functions can make to him under your management. This means you will have to quantify the reduced or avoided costs together with the productivity gains you can bring to the facility. If you are proposing to be a category manager for a consumer packaged-goods retailer, you must be prepared to prove the enhanced contribution one of his product categories can make to him under your management. This means you will have to quantify the expanded revenues and earnings, along with any reduced costs, you can bring to the category.

Containing the Costs of Certainty

In return for being given exclusivity in the management of some of a customer's assets as an outsourcer, you must expect to pay a price. The price can take several forms. To your normal costs of doing business, you will have to add the incremental costs of doing business as an exclusive supplier. Some of these costs are direct. The remainder are opportunity costs.

Your incremental costs will be only partially financial. In many cases the monetary portion of the costs will be the smaller and less meaningful part. The larger and more important share—of more lasting implication because of its potential impact on the future of your organization and operations—can make itself felt in many different ways. The sum of these costs will add up to you *costs of certainty*.

There are six common categories of certainty costs:

1. *Dedicated facility*. Customers may want you to set aside a trained management team, work force, office, or exclusive plant facility. They will want it to be immune from interruption or contamination by your work for other customers and may come to regard your dedicated organization as virtually their own.
2. *R&D help*. Customers may want your research and development capabilities to help their own R&D to create new products and processes. They may want to influence your top-level technical people to work in pursuit of customer competitive objectives rather than your own.
3. *Product specifications*. Customers may want you to manufacture customized products that are tailored to their own specifications. They may want a large degree of product control, the right to influence what goes into the product as well as what performance values come out of it.
4. *Inventory management*. Customers may want you to manage their inventory on a just-in-time basis, so that their carrying and handling costs can be minimized, with a managed reserve held for them at your expense "just in case."
5. *Application services*. Customers may want you to contribute skilled applications know-how to their own use of your products or to help their customers.
6. *Cost control*. Customers may want you to maximize the cost management of every aspect of your work in their dedicated facilities, constraining all unnecessary costs at the industry-standard level or below. They may want the right to impose their own cost control management systems if your costs get out of hand.

Resolving the Control Conundrum

Facility management and category management are not strategies to run your customers' businesses for them. They are strategies to help customers run their businesses better as a result of partnering with you.

When you take on the role of facilities manager, a customer entrusts all or part of one of his critical success functions to you. In order to relieve the customer of the costs and concerns of operating the function, you agree to manage the assets he owns or relieve him of the need to own the assets at all. For example, you may purchase the customer's assets outright or with a low-interest loan. From that point on, it becomes your job to guarantee that an optimal system is always under your management.

By partnering with you as a facility manager, a customer releases his management talent and financial resources from the facility for reinvestment elsewhere. Kodak calculated that it has unburdened itself of 40 percent of its telecommunications costs since DEC has been managing its facilities and is saving 50 percent in annual data center costs over and above IBM's management fee.

Today's customers are allying with facility managers in data processing, telecommunications, and retailing. Tomorrow's customers will broaden the range of operations they put up for outsourcing, contracting for outside asset management wherever the assets are costly, subject to rapid technological depreciation or require highly specialized management resources. The freed-up capital, plus freedom from the hassle of trying to bulldoze annual expenditure requests through the bureaucratic approval process, are attractive inducements to customers when they are combined with the reduced costs that are also made available.

What does a customer surrender to a facility or category manager?

He immediately gives up direct costs that can be accounted for more accurately on the outside. He gives up opportunity costs that can be converted into revenues. He gives up the allocation of his scarcest resource, management time and talent, to running operations that are not at the heart of his business but are supportive of it.

In spite of these advantages, facility management and category management may not be perceived as ideal solutions for every customer. Some managers will prefer to retain operating control of what they deem to be critical competitive assets rather than cede it to a third party, no matter how much more controlled their profit contributions can be.

In health care, where systems integration is becoming popular in inventory control, suppliers like Baxter International manage, order, and deliver multisupplier product mixes on a just-in-time basis to their partner hospitals. Baxter bypasses hospital inventory storerooms and loading docks to deliver directly to operating rooms and nursing floors where the users are. By "going stockless," hospitals outsource their warehousing operations to a supplier like Baxter on an exclusive basis. Savings accrue from the elimination of inventory and its associated costs, staff reductions, and the ability to convert storerooms to patient care and other money-making uses. Baxter benefits from being able to assess higher fees, taking about 30 percent of the savings and letting its partners pick up the remaining 70 percent. In this way, the margin-debilitating effects of product bidding are removed from suppliers while their customers also save. For every dollar spent to buy a product, hospitals have traditionally spent up to $3 to move it through their systems.

Yet, in spite of demonstrable benefits in cost-effectiveness, paleolithic attitudes still prevail. Some hospital administrators prefer to suffer unnecessary costs than worry that suppliers would write themselves larger orders than a hospital needs, or lose a sense of control by having nonemployees working in such a sensitive area as ordering supplies. Managers like these see their hospitals as hen houses and regard suppliers as foxes who are not to be let in.

Yet a customer's sense of the control of his internal operations is often more perceptual than real. At Kodak, it has been retrospectively said in regard to its information technology systems: "We only thought we had control. We used to spend two weeks per year on capital issues, competing for resources. Now we don't buy capital anymore. We can devote those two additional weeks to strategic issues of integrating technology with our

businesses and leveraging information systems as a corporate
asset."

Managing the Buy-Don't-Make Decision

Managing a customer facility or category will radically alter the
nature of your deliverables. While you will still be a supplier of
products and services, you will essentially supply management
skills that can maximize a customer operation's profit contribution. A supplier-as-manager works from a different capability
base than a supplier-as-manufacturer. Units of information become more important than product units. The profit contribution
of an entire customer facility or business category, rather than
only the contribution made by your products, becomes the drive
force of your relationship.

The importance of your products, whatever form they take,
will be progressively diminished. Coincidentally, the importance
of support services to make your products profitable will increase. The most critical service for you to provide is training to
make sure that your customers' people squeeze the full productivity out of every customer system you affect, whether you
manage it for them or help them manage it themselves.

Once a customer relinquishes the traditional need to manage
all his businesses and business functions by himself, he can
regard facility and category management as a common make-or-
buy decision. In tomorrow's competition, few companies will
make everything they sell. Nor will they manage every function
they operate. The same criterion will prevail: Who does it best,
us or them?

Tomorrow's customers will continually plan and replan their
management options as well as their manufacturing alternatives
in search of their "commercial cores," the smallest number of
products they must manufacture and the smallest number of
operations they must manage. In both cases, the eventual number
will be few rather than many. What are our noncritical businesses, they will ask, the mature commodities that generate only
cash flow, not profits? Would they be marketable at a profit by an
outsourcer without our costs or distractions? What are our non-

critical functions, the processes where we have no proprietary know-how? Are their contributions obtainable more cost-effectively from an outsourcer?

Facility management and category management are data-dependent strategies. Without three kinds of knowledge, no supplier—no matter how superior his products may be—can pretend to be able to manage a customer's facility. On the other hand, a facility manager does not need product superiority. His superiority must be elsewhere, in what he knows.

What You Must Know About Your Customers

You must know the current contribution to customer value that is being made by the customer operations or categories that you affect. What is their contribution to total customer costs? What are they contributing to revenues and earnings? How do these contributions compare to a customer's industry norms, to his key competitors' norms, and to the trend of his own corporate norms averaged over the past three to five years?

You must know the customer's business objective for each operation or category. Does he need to improve its contribution? If so, by how much and how soon? How much of a priority is it for him—enough to warrant the investment that will be required to have you integrate and manage his system? Are you the most competent manager to maximize the return he will get from his investment?

You must know the customer's operating managers. How partnerable are they likely to be with you? Do they already have a preferred partner? How do they work: Is their operating culture conservative or venturesome, are they committed to be on the leading edge or are they followers, and are they more likely to focus on the investment they are required to make with you and treat it as a cost or will they be more concerned with its return?

These areas of knowledge are the keys to understanding each customer's operations. They tell you whether or not you can do business and what kind of business you can probably do. Will you be able to propose yourself to a customer as his most cost-effective manager? Or will you be able to consult only in a more limited, vertical aspect of his business or simply vend?

What You Must Know About Your Own Business

You must know the dollar values your products, services, and systems can contribute to a customer. You must know how much value you normally contribute to reducing a customer's costs or increasing his revenues in the operations of his business that you affect. You must also know how soon your contributions normally show their results.

These areas of knowledge are the keys to understanding your business. They tell you why you are in business. They also tell your customers why they must outsource their business to you.

What You Must Know About Your Competitors

You must know the value that can be added to your own products and services by the products and services of your competitors. Which of their products, integrated with your own, adds the greatest value to your contribution or causes your value to flow sooner? What is the optimal configuration of each multi-supplier system of products and services that will yield a customer the lowest life-cycle cost and the highest efficiency for each dollar he invests?

These areas of knowledge are the keys to understanding your competitors' businesses. Unless you know their businesses, you are unable to know whether or how to integrate their products and services. If you cannot be an integrator of them, you can only be a vendor of your own products. As such, you will be vulnerable to a competitor who can integrate your own products into a megasystem of his own configuration that he will manage for your customers. No matter how impressive your product values, he will be able to offer a value superior to yours because your values will be included in it.

The Nostalgia
of the Man
From Coca-Cola

The man from Coca-Cola stood by his office window and, although apparently looking out, looked back. I wonder, he mused aloud, if we will ever again see the simplicity in business that we had for so many years before there was all this competition, when we had one basic product in one size in one package that was recognizable all over the world and sold, at least here in the United States, at one price.

I suppose, he said, the days are gone forever when Jell-O came in only "six delicious flavors" that everybody knew were strawberry, raspberry, cherry, orange, lemon, and lime and when there were just the Big Three car manufacturers and all the General Motors cars were either Chevrolets, Pontiacs, Buicks, Oldsmobiles, or Cadillacs. Wouldn't it be wonderful if we could relive those times?

He may get his wish. The microniching of markets will continue to drive product proliferation. But in many other respects, tomorrow's competition will be less than today's. Industry consolidations will leave fewer players to compete. Alliances will make competition a group affair, leaving fewer competitors. Customers who practice facility management and category management will replace product competition in many categories by selecting one or two prime suppliers on a dedicated, exclusive basis. Where old-style selling still prevails, competing on value will change the nature of competition as well as who can compete. Any number of product vendors could once compete on price. Only one or two suppliers will be able to propose the most compelling values.

In the 1970s and 1980s, the basic competitive problem was "getting in." In tomorrow's competition, there will be two problems. One will be getting in first. If that fails, the other will be getting your competitor out. If he is practicing lateral leadership, co-managing and competing on value, there may be no way to get him out until he or his customer undergoes a destabilizing change.

Getting into a business first, or strategically allying with a customer first, requires you to forsake nostalgia for "simplicity in business" and become aware of how the competitive complexion in your industry can change, sometimes overnight, to your disadvantage. When disequilibrium occurs today, it almost always comes from the outside. This will be even more likely tomorrow. An outsider is someone who has nothing to gain from nostalgia. When he strikes, a domino effect occurs as all the erstwhile competitors in a field become noncompetitive at one and the same time and for the same reason.

Fountain pen manufacturers become noncompetitive when ballpoint technology made them obsolete. Ballpoint pens did not come from any of the leading manufacturers of fountain pens. Electric calculators made adding machines noncompetitive. They were not invented by any of the leading makers of electromechanical office products. Videogames were not invented by the makers of board games. Semiconductors were not invented by the makers of vacuum tubes or transistors. Radial tires were not invented by the major American rubber manufacturers. Diet soda did not come from either of the two major cola companies. Overnight package delivery was not invented by the major airlines or parcel delivery services. In every case, the traditional competitors were nostalgically devoted to protecting their franchises rather than renewing them.

There is a lesson to be learned about letting yesterday's thinking obscure tomorrow's thinking from the experience of Edson de Castro of Data General Corporation. Looking at every company's history as a succession of innovative waves, de Castro has said that "few companies are able to participate in the next wave" because they are blinded by the business at hand. In de Castro's case, he stayed too long with minicomputers, putting his resources into making them work better and cost less, while the next wave of personal computers passed him by. "My biggest mistake was failing to get Data General into the PC business."

Winning tomorrow's competition means starting to compete today as if it were already tomorrow. With each day of delay, your markets have a better chance of being niched, your most growable customers may be partnered by competitive growers, and the customer managers of the facilities that you affect or the categories of their businesses that you sell into may contract with other outsourcers. Your suppliers who can grow you best may become partnered with someone else. A competitor may make a series of toehold investments that effectively freezes you out of an emergent technology or he may establish an armlock on your market by setting himself up as its standard of value.

A year from now, will you be next year's Man from Coca-Cola standing by your office window and, although looking out, will you look back?

Dec. 5/99 Sunday life insurance

Motivating I A'm to do business
with their firms through their

I. S.

i e how to add 250K
to your girl

Index

advertising industry, 18
Aetna Life & Casualty Company, 98
A. G. Edwards, Inc., 105
Airbus Industrie, 76
aircraft manufacturing industry, 147–148, 155–156
Air France, 95, 146
airline industry, 19, 95, 146
Air Products & Chemicals, Inc., 27–28
Akers, John, 13–14, 137
American Airlines, 95
American Can Company, 30, 69
American Telephone and Telegraph (AT&T), 11, 17, 39
American Telephone & Electronics Company, 36
Anders, William, 118
Anderson, Ed, 42
Anheuser-Busch, 31, 57
Apollo (computer company), 12
Apple Computer, 22, 38, 135–136
  Claris software division of, 29
  dealer specialization in, 104

innovation in, 91–92
  in research and development partnerships, 149
Applied Intelligent Systems, 151
ASEA, 44
Ashton-Tate, 149–150
automobile industry
  Ford–TRW alliance in, 158–159
  future cooperation in, 140–141
  globalism in, 95–96
  innovation in, 76
  joint ventures in, 148–149
  manufacturing partnerships in, 147
  retailing in, 17
  tires in, 105

Baldwin Locomotive Works, 11
banking industry, 18, 43, 96
Baxter International, 169
BBC Brown Boveri, 44
B. Dalton Bookseller, 20
B. F. Goodrich, 26–27, 44, 52
biotechnology industry, 142–143
Birmingham Steel Corporation, 27

177